Casualty

W · W · NORTON & COMPANY · NEW YORK · LONDON

Casualty

Corinne Browne

LC 80-84897

W. W. Norton & Company, Inc. 500 Fifth Avenue, New York, N.Y. 10110
W. W. Norton & Company Ltd. 25 New Street Square, London EC4A 3NT

ISBN 0 393 01422 3

1 2 3 4 5 6 7 8 9 0

For Robert

and

Joshua and Lila

It is not unusual that the old bury the young, though it is an abomination to nature.

"In Memoriam," Nikki Giovanni

The whole experience has been difficult and saddening for all of us. There is a great temptation to leave things alone in hopes that the anguish will abate, and that further developments will not introduce further complications or tragedies. What I am saying is that one cannot help but fear to some extent that the book you are creating will in some way be painful.

Doug Westphall

Acknowledgments

This book was begun at the Wurlitzer Foundation and a good portion of it was written at the MacDowell Colony.

I am grateful to Happy and Ken Price for sharing their part of New Mexico with me.

I would like to thank Rachel Michaud for her help and encouragement and Carol Houck Smith for her skillful editing.

Casualty

One

At the far end of the room the old man mixed canned vegetables with shredded pieces of Spam and put them into plastic bowls. "Come and eat," he said.

Night had fallen into the valley. I turned my back on it and went to the table. Between our places he put a bottle of Chablis mixed with rosé. "Wine?" he asked as he poured it.

The old man bent over his bowl, ate silently and quickly, as though he were insatiable. He rarely spoke while he was eating. Gray hairs grew out of his ears. I dug down through wax beans and Spam to iceburg lettuce. I tried to sit calmly, to readjust to the sounds, to the sense of northern New Mexico. My heart hammered from the altitude and from the feeling I always get when I see the chapel which stands outside the hut where we were eating.

I had flown from New York, driven over the mountains

from the town of Taos, in the direction of the village called Eagle Nest. I had raced to get here. I wanted to see the old man. I was looking for a way to tell his story and I was going to stay until I found it.

He washed his food down with a swallow of wine, leaned back, and filled his pipe. He seemed content to be watching over the chapel, which he had made in memory of his son, and which he guarded and fussed over. He often remarked that he wished he, too, could have gone to Vietnam where his son, a lieutenant in the Marine Corps, had died in combat at Con Thien. "I could have kept up with the best of them," he liked to say, sitting in the hut up there on the knoll.

Firelight made scratching fingers on the boarded-up windows; wind tore at the walls as though the mountains had fired it to uproot the hut; draughts bled into the room; nothing creaked. It might have been a bunker or a cave.

The story of how the monument had come to replace the old man's son had fascinated me for too long. It stuck to me; I kept finding bits of it all over me, like burrs. It kept me coming back to this godforsaken spot, sometimes traveling thousands of miles, just to be there. I have been there at all hours and in all seasons. The wind always blows. It claps the rope against the flagpole, clangs it with an eerie echoing sound.

The chapel is made of white stucco and it lifts, like a wing, off a promontory overlooking the long Moreno Valley, beneath the Sangre de Cristo—the Blood of Christ—Mountains. In the daytime it looks like a ship's prow, riding

over the valley. At night, swathed in light, it looks like a
ghost's arm, pointing out the stars.

After his son was buried, the old man's wife thought of
erecting a memorial. His remaining son said that he would
help in whatever way he could. They decided to build a
chapel for all veterans of Vietnam. The old man commis-
sioned a young architect to do the plans. His only request
was that no one should leave the monument feeling as he
had before about peace and war. He never said how he
wanted them to feel, but the chapel is a landmark to the
changes in his own life.

In the past few years more than 100,000 people have
driven up the steep road and stopped outside the stark
building. Some of them stay in their cars, afraid or angry or
just halted. Others step along the flat white steppingstones
which lead past rows of plain white markers with the names
of the dead—

Denver Berkheimer	Jay Mitchell
Ohio	Oklahoma
Rolando Hernandez	Alejandro Diaz
Texas	New York

and go inside where it is dim and cool. A naked cross rises in
the structure's bow. On the wall behind, thirteen uniformed
men stare out of photographs. The old man's son is always at
their center. I cannot tell from his picture what kind of
person he was.

Some visitors speak to the old man. Some complain that
there is no bathroom. Others tell him about their lives, ask

him about the chapel. A young man who comes all the way from Albuquerque said to him, "You know, this is my church."

An elderly woman from the old man's town came, looked, and said, disdainfully, "Where's the chapel? It doesn't mean anything at all to me."

Once, when he had been away from the chapel for a while, the old man returned and found a crudely lettered sign by the door: "Why did you lock me out when I needed to come in?"

Many people walk around and go away without saying much. Some, like me, go away and return. Quite a few say nothing, because they are crying.

I know of no other monument like it in this country.

I first went to the chapel in 1972, the year I lived in New Mexico. The Vietnam war was still going on. By then I had met men who had gone to jail because they believed the war was immoral, and men in an army hospital who had lost their limbs in the war; I knew men who could no longer work or think or love or even cry because of the war. I had changed a great deal during the war. I had grown up curious, spoiled, and comfortable; I had become disillusioned, uncomfortable, and political. Every time I went to the chapel, I thought about all of these things, and when I was driving home to Taos over the mountains, I would stop the car, get out, and walk around and around. I always felt I was on the verge of figuring out something important.

It was the sense of being on that verge which kept me going back to the chapel, even after I no longer lived in New Mexico. It was why I was eating in the hut with the old man that night, in late November, 1974.

At that time, in addition to managing the chapel, the old man was working at the ranch he used to own near the memorial. After his son died, his wife wouldn't live at the ranch anymore, so they sold it and moved to a town called Springer, sixty miles away. They reserved a portion of the ranch, just enough land for the chapel.

He built the hut which served as an office and as a place for him to stay overnight sometimes. I was determined to sleep there, so he had offered me his bed and agreed to stay at the ranch. I don't know exactly why I wanted to spend the night—in my mind it was part of a pilgrimage. I thought it might solve the mystery, clarify the power of the place. I thought it might be my last chance to pick the burrs off me, get them into a clump, so that I could throw them, so that I could tell, even in a song, about the old man, his wife, their sons, and the chapel.

•   •   •

"What do you think of the lights?" he asked. "We didn't have them the last time you were here." Highpowered lights set around the chapel made it gleam like a crooked phantom finger over the black valley. I had nearly run off the road when I saw it that evening, and I told him so. He nodded and sighed, the way he often did. He always seemed to mourn each advance, as though it were never enough.

"I have a pain," he pushed his index finger into the center of his chest. "Right here. I don't know what it is. Tension, maybe."

He had had a heart attack after his son died, and when he

recovered, he had started running. I knew about the pain in his chest and the blood in his stool. I knew he'd change his work boots for sneakers and run the next day, six miles in the blistering wind before sunrise, running to be alive.

He put on his glasses and stared at me. "I have to keep going."

He had recounted a greal deal of his life to me, but I didn't know him at all. I had never been sure what his purpose was in talking to me, but I knew he had one because he always has one.

"Can't you let up a little?" I asked.

Why not, I wondered. He had wrenched himself off a farm in Wisconsin, battled his way through the Depression, served in the Pacific; he had built houses in Albuquerque, taught history, and earned the Ph.D. that dubbed him Doctor. He had written books and, finally, flailed away at the chapel, which rose fifty feet into the air outside the hut—a wild gesture of longing for something lost, and of mourning for that loss.

Why couldn't he be serene, the way old men are supposed to be? Why couldn't he let the wind play against his palms, instead of smashing at it with his fists? Anger, like a mean little boil, broke out in me.

He answered my question by shuffling through some papers and producing a worn newspaper article. "Dr. Victor Westphall . . ." it began, and went on to say that he held the Southwestern regional record in weight lifting—dead lift 464 pounds; body 148 pounds—for men of his age in northern New Mexico. I put it down, mumbled something approving. His passion for physical fitness baffled me.

We cleared the table and sat down by the fire. He smoked his pipe and I smoked a cigarette. When I finished, he asked if I wanted to go into the chapel. I didn't really, but there was a plea in his tone, so I said I wanted to go. He crossed the room to the outsized tape machine and turned it on. He slid open the glass door, and we stepped into the icy wind, as "Jesu, Joy of Man's Desiring" blared into the darkness that lay outside the circle of light.

We walked through the doorway and he switched on the lights inside the chapel. Its starkness hit me. Being inside the chapel is like being inside a bleached bone. There is no quirk, no solace. On one side a horizontal slit eyes the valley. Behind the cross a vertical slash looks out at the mountains. The steps that lead down to the cross are wide and cold. Behind us the thirteen photographs of dead men hung on the wall like family portraits. David Westphall, wearing dress blues, was in the center. He was twenty-eight years old when he died.

I turned toward the old man, needing the sight of flesh. He was moving up and down the line of photographs. Beneath the music I heard him murmuring, "Good boys, I be back in the morning, sleep well, boys. . . ."—a kind of baby talk. He glanced at me sheepishly. "I like to say goodnight to them when I'm here."

He shut the door and we made our way back to the hut. He told me that there was someone down at the ranch he'd like me to meet, that if it was all right, he'd go down and try to find him. He looked at his watch and said it was early; it might take awhile to find the person, but they would be back. I had never met anyone there before, and I couldn't imagine who it would be. He seemed so eager that I had to agree. He is a man who gets his way.

He went out and I paced in front of the fire. I felt the resentment of the traveler robbed of anonymity, the one whose plane or train trip is invaded by a chatterer. I had planned to be alone. I wanted to sit in the wind-battered bunker and think about the dead son, the father and mother, the puzzles and convolutions of their lives and mine. I didn't want to talk to anyone.

I had been pulled back there, like a fish on a line that silvered out across a thousand miles, drawing me back, never quite leaving me in peace, tugging at me even in my sleep. Once, trying to fathom it, I had underlined Don Juan's words about places of power. "And thus one could develop strange and injurious ties with a locale. Those ties anchor a man to a place of power, sometimes for a lifetime." He was talking about people who were "disturbed," people who could be "drained" by these places. I didn't know if I was disturbed in those terms, but sometimes I believed that the attraction was unnatural, and I longed to be done with it. The thought that I might not be able to break the tie, to drain the power the place had over me, terrified me.

There was a telephone in the hut, and I thought of calling home. I needed to hear my children's voices, but it would be later there, and they would be asleep. I thought of calling a friend, but there would be no way to explain what I was doing. There would be no way to say that I felt I was sitting in the cup of solitude. It would sound ludicrous to say, "I'm here, in this unearthly setting, to find out why I'm here." I wore out the possibilities of voices one by one, until I was left with my own.

Two

I grew up in the suburb of a big midwestern city. The people in the city called the suburb the Lake. They were envious. Our neighborhood was all-white Protestant—English or German—and we were the only ones with a French name. Actually, there was one Jewish family; they were in hardware, but I think they were sorry they had come to live there. My friends' fathers were executives in flour mills and grain companies. They hunted, fished, and played tennis and golf. In the winter they raced each other on the lake in iceboats. My father was an officer in a savings bank, and he didn't do any of those things.

Our house was right on the lake. There was the lawn and three old cedar trees, leaning together, right on the edge of the lake. When the wind blew the snow off the ice, we used to put on our skates, hold up umbrellas, and go like hell until we couldn't stand the cold. In the summer we went out the back door, jumped off the dock, and swam around the lake to see our friends.

At school they told us about the Indians and we sent them clothes and money. I heard about the reservations, but it was so clean and comfortable where we lived that it was hard for me to imagine what the life of the Indians was like.

I learned about patriotism in my father's bathroom/ dressing room. He had a long couch with a red plastic mat on it. He used to close the toilet seat and sit on it, put me across his knees, and spank me for not obeying his rules. On the wall behind the toilet was a picture of one of the destroyers which had helped America win the Second World War. On the ceiling was wallpaper which had pictures of fighter planes. The bathroom, altogether, was red, white, and blue.

Most of the men at the Lake had gone to the War. My father had had hemorrhaging ulcers and they wouldn't take him. So he worked for the Red Cross, but he never got over missing the War. If I asked him now how he felt about it, he'd say he felt nothing. But I'm sure he still does.

We were patriotic. We ate all our food and we said the pledge of allegiance at school. When I was thirteen, I vowed that I wouldn't be like my mother. That meant that I didn't want to stay in the cellophane bag, didn't want to spend my life driving children around and drinking martinis. But I didn't think of not being an American. I felt somehow at the center, really American, and I thought that we were tall and strong and good.

Years later, as I was driving toward Taos after a failed marriage, I wasn't so sure about the good. I was only sure that my children and I had to keep going from one place to another, crossing one border after another, until we found something. If I had said to myself while we were crossing those borders, "I am in mourning for my illusions," I would have answered, "What an ass!" But because I had lost them, I felt violated.

I had the disease of the road, the national itch which passed from the pioneers down through Jack Kerouac and on to us who inherit it. When you travel, you see it. On every thruway, freeway, highway, and road they're there: hitchers and bikers, campers, motor homes, mobile homes and, like a new breed of gypsy machines, huts perched on the back of pick-ups, old buses, or beat-up trucks stuffed with kids and older-than-kids, long hair, frizzed hair, swaddled in ninth-hand dresses, shirts, serapes, and shawls, washed in collective scents—incense, dope, and patchouli—scorning the things their parents mortgaged their minds for, doing without the things they used to have, in order to stay on the move. They don't have a generational premium on it, either. Their dads and granddads are steadfastly driving their Wanderers and Discoverers, their Apaches and Roadrunners—those tidy miniature worlds-on-wheels—from town to town, from campground to campground. Couples retire, sell their houses, store their stuff, climb in their Airstreams, and go. Some of them band together, cross continents in caravans. Older people in other countries look up from their rosebushes in dismay when they hear about this phenomenon. They work to earn a rest; we work to earn flight.

My children and I had chosen, this time, a whimsical route that ran, essentially, from Montreal to New Mexico.

My recollections begin in the middle of America.

In Jordan, Minnesota, we sat in a clean, dark café, in a sea of signs:

WE DUST OUR PIES EVERY DAY

YOUR FACE IS GOOD
BUT WE CAN'T GET IT
IN THE CASH REGISTER

IT'S HARD TO GET RICH
IN A SMALL TOWN
EVERYBODY'S
WATCHING

The pies were good and everybody watched us eat them. Still, we felt warmed, touched by rusticity, reassured. How bad can things be, after all, as long as there are these silo towns, these cafés, these simple, elbow-jabbing, hee-hawing signs?

And farther south, in Hinckley, where the old highway lies empty and cracking, the farmers at Hoppy's kept their striped denim caps on, dug into their man's meat portions, their mashed potatoes with gravy-in-a-pocket. I kept my eye on the farmers while I ate, because the woman in the loose, flowered dress at the next table had a terrible brown crust all over her hands.

The Grace Hotel, four dollars a night for a cabin, how can you beat it? We didn't mind that there was an outhouse with a door that didn't latch, that the walls of the room were pale blue and dusty, cracked and cobwebby. That there were no curtains, no soap, and a large spider in the sink. We lay in the metal bed and listened to the baseball game nearby, the scratch of the chokecherry against the rusty screen, the chorus of crickets, and the train which slowed, and whistled, and passed on.

It felt fine to be on solid ground, midway between New York City and L.A., to see people there, working, farming, walking, dying, instead of the ghosts they are made to seem by the drunkards and missionaries who "represent" them in the cloakrooms on that little rise in Washington, D.C. It also felt good because we didn't have to stay.

The road disease does not allow staying; it does, however cultivate odd pictures which become memories. We stopped at the Walker Art Gallery in Minneapolis. I remember the Matisses which were on exhibit; mostly I remember the young woman with brown braids, a white blouse, and denim cut-offs standing in front of a drawing of dancers. She was leaning slightly on crutches, one long tanned leg firmly planted. The other leg of her shorts was empty.

And I remember the surreal sense I got when, days later and nowhere in South Dakota, we saw the first sign for the Reptile Gardens, three hundred miles away. And, in Cheyenne, Wyoming, succumbing to the perversity of the road, we pulled into Little America, the world's largest gasoline station with fifty-six pumps and a stuffed penguin which "couldn't survive the trip so it was sent east to be stuffed." We even ate at Little America, bleary-eyed amidst pink lights and hundreds of enormous stuffed animals, toys trinkets soaps puzzles baskets bags purses pillows shirts T-shirts pajamas plaques signs banners pennants and blankets which all said Cheyenne, Wyoming. We sat silently amidst the faces of depraved Americans on summer maneuvers. Our waitress was very angry with us for being there so we gulped our cheeseburgers and scuttled past the fifty-six shining pumps back to our car.

The road, of course, exacts its price: days of alienation and despair. The highway sucks you along, you are silent, you don't want to stop, you don't want to go on. Your eyes burn, your neck aches, you wish for home, whatever that may be. You think for hours about how nice it would be to stretch out your legs. You long for the next town, but when you get there you are afraid to stop. You wonder how long you can do it before you snap. You stop to sleep.

We slept in a desolate town, in a nameless hotel where old men sat in a lobby full of plastic flowers. At Wall Drug in Wall, South Dakota, I asked for toothpaste and the woman said, "Halfway down on the west wall." I wondered: Are people planted here, or do they yearn east or westward? How did it come to be a human fate to have been dropped off here in the seed of an exhausted ancestor? Teen-agers drove around and around in unwilling cars.

We rode through the plains, mile upon mile of planted fields, corn and wheat, potatoes and sugar beet. We were in the land of blue-green light. The highway ran off the horizon like pale, giant tiretracks. Mirages rose off the asphalt, and we spoke of the Wizard of Oz.

Some days we followed the old highways which usually run parallel to the faster interstates. They were narrow and full of bumps, but they ran us past the old houses, America's ruins. If a foreigner asked me what to see in this country, I would say, go and look at the abandoned houses. They have faces. The cars, the tractors, the furniture and families are gone, and, in their place, are the faces. We got out, sometimes, and walked around them, sat in their yards, or peered in their windows. Hours passed and we didn't notice, so totally was time drowned out by their silence. I saw their expressions change with the time of day.

We stopped on old Highway 40, somewhere near Grainfield, Kansas. There was dew on the grass that had grown right up to the front door. The house was awake and waiting for its people, for bacon to fry, for milk to pour, like a lost dog, still full of expectancy, unsuited for solitude. Pale sunlight tapped at the upstairs windows which seemed to call out for children.

By noon the house had hunkered down under the blistering sun. It looked like an eruption on the shadowless land, like a wart on all the green that grew relentlessly around it. It had no place and it had no function; the hour belonged to the freight train that lumbered by, to the trucks that rolled toward town, to the Rainbirds that swept the fields, ceaselessly watering the country's sustenance. We waited in the heat, feeling like the house, heavy and antediluvian.

We lay under a tree and watched the afternoon drift towards twilight. Sparrows chatted amongst the dead lilacs. Starlings swooped. Shadows from trees, from the eaves tricked us, and the graciousness of the house deceived us. Faces passed old glass in the windows, footsteps creaked on floor boards. The breeze brought us whispers from the fireside, telling of the walk to town in winter, of the first rain in drought years, of children born in their father's bed, of snakes and blackberries, of rusting tools, of mortgages, of the first TV, of the Greyhound, of corporations that sucked up the land, of leaving. We went away, not speaking.

Grainfield, "A Community with Pride," looked deserted at the end of day. Just houses, churches, a few trailers, a gas station near a streetlight which went on as we watched it. At the edge of town the town ended abruptly. The plains were like the ocean. Far away a grain silo gleamed like a galleon.

We sat in the café. The man who served us wore his tattoos like sleeves. He asked us how we came to be in such an out-of-the-way place; most folks, he said, don't get off the interstate. We said we were just wandering and he shook his head. The thruway has no exit for Grainfield, and no one with brains in his head would drive along Highway 40. It would have been too complicated to explain that if you stay on the interstate you never get to Grainfield.

As we despaired of the plains, the Badlands began. The hills were ochre and deep lavender, worked into spires and columns and cylinders, shot through with holes, caves, gullies, and gulches. About three-quarters of the way up, remaining at the same level, lay a pink stripe. The earth was like the Hinckley woman's crusted hands. I felt drugged, or mildly deranged.

Later, in the Rockies, I felt the same loss of control of my senses, although there it had more to do with form than with color. We stopped in the foothills for coffee, cantaloupe, and trout. Then we began to climb. A mule deer stood in a bog by a river. We stopped, waded through the freezing water, climbed up and lay half-nude in the sun on the damp pine needles. All around us sat the elephant-hide mountains; elk

were feeding on their sides. Before we could dress the rain
came, then the hail, and before we reached the river the sun
had returned. Rainbows came and went like clouds.

We slept at the Blue Spruce, a log cabin beside a stream.
In the morning I picked small purple daisies and put them in
a paper cup on the outdoor table and we had oranges, eggs,
and bacon there in the high grass filled with clover. I
thought, why don't we find a real estate agent, cash in our
last traveler's checks, and build a cabin? Why shouldn't we
stay awhile? Then the man who owned the place came by
and asked if we'd like to see the colt he and his daughter had
delivered during the night. The mare was eating peacefully;
the colt nursed, shifting his stilt legs. The man grinned, said
he'd told his daughter they should name it Half-Wino, because "he walks like a drunk and has a kinky tail like a
nigger." We packed up and got back on the road. I consoled
myself that nature, after all, is an escape.

The road has ways of making up for its disappointments.
In Hill City, South Dakota, after the children were asleep, I
strolled up the old streets, sniffing the night mountain air,
went on into the Lit'l Nashville. Sawdust covered the floor,
Schlitz fishing lures beamed on the walls, and the band
played polkas, waltzes, and square dances. I drank draft
beer and pretty soon everyone was clapping, diving for the
oyster, digging for the clam. A young GI in fatigues stomped
around in the circle; his eyes were shining; he was sweating
and a little drunk. The music, the beer, and the soldier made
me feel breathless, the way dancing did when I was eigh-
teen, and I thought it would go on and on. The walls were
plastered with lithographs of Wild Bill Hickok, Calamity

Jane, Kit Carson. Their names are exciting; we do not know how desperate their lives were. We buy the glamour from script writers who leave their mark by oiling the myths. We shiver in front of these pictures of hangings, thrill to the harshness of eye-for-an-eye justice. Our lack of hard knowledge permits us our nostalgia. In a sense, we are a history-less and disjointed nation, and that is why we hold to our illusions.

In school my children make birchbark *tipis* and cardboard covered wagons. When I have extra money I buy old quilts, marvel at the clarity which prompted women to take dead-men's clothes and sew them into future warmth they called mourning quilts. But we don't get to the underside of it all. When I read that in 1909 a man who moved from Arkansas to the Chisos Mountains lost six hundred of his horses and colts to mountain lions, I have to shrug because there is no way I can make sense of such an event. We cannot fathom past tragedies or other people's present ones because our energy is sapped by hiding from our own. Our highways bypass our ghettos.

The road took us to Mesa Verde in southern Colorado— the town hacked out of cliffs by people who simply disappeared—took us past graves and monuments and In-dian lands and into towns where shops wanted our coins. It didn't yet take us to South Valley, outside Albuquerque, where a man who has grass outside his home is considered rich because he can afford to water it. Adobe South Valley, where there are no sidewalks or streetlights, no paved roads or sewage system. Where the dogs are gaunt and the harsh winds raise no dust from the obdurate land. Where old people live on leftover gravy. Where our recession, or depression, or whatever we choose to call it, has been their reality for years. As long as you keep moving you never have to sit down with the fact that we may not be as tall and as strong and as good as we think we are.

We were nearly in New Mexico so we slowed down. We invented reasons to linger in Colorado. We slept in the old hotel in Durango. We prowled through shops full of the same original authentic handmade Indian turquoise-and-silver jewelry we had seen for hundreds of miles before. I took our bluejeans to a laundromat and thought about having the car serviced. The road is an addiction and it is hard to face the cure. I put off our destination as though it were the plague. I dreaded the inevitable postroad blues, and languished in our dwindling Kerouakian days.

We sat at a scarred picnic table at a rest stop along the highway. Trucks, like behemoths, thundered by. The trash can near the table overflowed with summer refuse. I wondered what I was doing there. I had made no friends, no enemies; I had been no one's guest or accomplice. But I imagined I was doing something important, something everyone should do. Once in a British travel agency I had seen a poster which said, "SEE AMERICA WHILE IT LASTS."

·   ·   ·

In the car I taught the children to sing, "Oh, the bear went over the mountain, the bear went over the mountain, the bear went over the mountain, to see what he could see." We sang it until we were hoarse, or until they went to sleep.

Three

In high summer 1972 we crossed the Colorado border. A green-and-white sign said that we were leaving Colorful Colorado; the sign welcoming us to New Mexico, Land of Enchantment, had fallen down.

We stopped and got out and looked at the fallen sign. I slid my foot up against it, as though it could reassure me that even though it had toppled over, maybe long ago, and no one knew or bothered to put it up again, it was safe to go on. We went on through tan, arid land. The highway seemed to exist for nothing. The few towns looked like tiny dumps in the desert—white, rust-streaked, one-pump gas stations, tired attendants with sullen eyes, teen-agers lying under sagging cars, greasing up escape. Main streets were lined with closed shops. In La Perdita we saw no one, not a face to register our passing, to let us know we were really there.

Occasionally there were signs for ranches—yes, of course, that's where the people were, on the ranches, with names like Cody and Bigelow as well as Torres and Orrego. Nothing to worry about. You are in America.

In the west the sun burned; in the east rain glided off the mountains in gray stripes. We watched the stripes move toward us and toward the sun, across the sand dunes. We stopped singing, talking, and fighting. It was as though we were holding our breath. Any sound beside the whirring of the wheels would have jeopardized the tiny place we held on the highway, a minute moving anchor in a shifting perspective. For more than a hundred miles there was no other car.

After what seemed a very long time, we stopped and got out at the bridge which crosses the Rio Grande, stared down into six hundred feet of echoing purple gorge which lies outside Taos. The brown river snaked along below. Paul Horgan wrote, "It is born of winter, this river, in one of the longest seasons of cold in the United States." It is born in the heights of the Rocky Mountains, but here it looked narrow and mean. A small dark-skinned boy climbed on all fours up the rocks toward us. In the bare parking lot beside the bridge a motor home, called the Pace Maker, was parked and a woman with a leathery face watched her husband watching the river. A hawk rode the wind farther out, over the buff-colored land spotted with cacti, sage, ocotillo, mesquite, and the rough deep-green piñon. He circled, his wings tipped up at the ends. All around us were mountains and mesas; it was as though we had driven into the center of a huge bowl. We got back into the car, crossed the Rio Grande, and drove on toward Taos.

My cousin, who lives there, had sent me a letter the previous winter. She had enclosed a sprig of sage and wrote about the New Mexico sunsets. I had kept an image of adobe courtyards, desert flowers, and ancient pueblos in a vault in my mind all the while we were crossing borders. Now we were nearly there. As far as the eye could see, there was no bright color, only the jagged mountains, flat tan land, the black road, with an occasional beer can glinting in the relentless sun.

People tisk and moan when they see beer cans lying around, lounging at the bottom of streams, bobbing up and down beneath waterfalls. I decided long ago that they are simply a part of the American landscape. Any painter who doesn't put them in, on beaches or in meadows, is a liar. But here, on Highway 111, heading straight for Taos, I ignored them because they weren't part of my plan.

I had decided that if I found a place which still had the qualities of a frontier land—physical difficulties without too much pollution or overcrowding—I would stop before I got to another border. I would put down roots. Of course, I realized it was impossible; I had left my roots behind, truncated. They had dried up in the cellophane bag. My god, how blindly, swiftly we leave before we are twenty, dying to pack up, stealing lying plotting whoring our way out, thinking of nothing day and night but the hour, the moment when we can kiss it all goodbye. It doesn't matter whether it's inherited, this malady of leaving, or whether it's an emblem of the times; the fact is we get on the road and don't look back. Only now I begin to remember, with a pang, the three cedar trees and the lake they no longer swim in because it has become a cesspool. Only today do I feel safe enough to say, it really doesn't matter that I don't know my own reality.

We drove past squat mud houses, dried-up fields with emaciated horses and cows lying under sparse shade trees. The sun was setting behind us and the Blood of Christ Mountains reflected its glare. I thought, I am not at home anywhere, but perhaps my children can put down roots here. Perhaps the place will bear enough human and earthly variety for them to wish to stay, or at least to return, and grow old here. And at the same time I said, oh Corinne, you're such a romantic, but I already knew that, and I didn't care.

In the west, it had seemed that people still had something to be patriotic about, their land was still worth fighting for, maybe even dying for. Children looked healthy. They survive the survivors—people who derived their substance from adventure, their power from adversity. I had read reports of prairie fires which reigned amongst the fiends that hounded covered wagons. One told of a wagon train which passed safely through a fire because of a favoring wind. At night the wind changed and the next day the flames devoured the entire caravan. I wanted to know that I would be that brave, or that determined, or that mad. I wanted something to be patriotic about, even if it was a desert plot.

In art history class I had seen slides of the pueblos—the most extraordinary living structures in North America, the professor had said. The landscape with its clumps of trees, arroyos, and adobe huts looked like a movie set. And the word "Taos" reverberated with names—Kit Carson, Mabel

Dodge Luhan, D. H. Lawrence, Willa Cather, Edward Curtis, Georgia O'Keeffe—and with history. Fifty years ago writers and artists had thrown themselves at the mercy of bad roads, drought, and treachery to go there, and some of them stayed. A hundred years ago mountain men—trappers and traders—had brought skins down from the north, exchanged them for currency which permitted them to stay awhile, siphon off some wine and women's warmth from the town. A thousand years ago Pueblo Indians chipped their towns out of cliffs beside the Rio Grande, warded off the Navajo, irrigated their corn and beans, and lived well without dreaming of light-skinned men an ocean and a continent away who would come, one day, selling crosses and filling pouches. Today stone axes lie under unmarked graves plowed beneath supermarkets. Commitments, animosities, and devotions lie on top of one another and must be deciphered along with the land. "Life," said Charles Lummis, "is the least vital feature of New Mexico." It is a place which has no ordinary monuments.

I felt as though we were driving into a story.

We slowed to a crawl as the highway turned into the main street of Taos. On one side were art galleries sporting paintings of Indians, cacti, coyotes, and matadors. On the other were hardware stores, cafés, and a J.C. Penney under a Spanish-style arcade. The street was choked with campers and tourist cars and, although the sun had gone down, the heat was thick and obscene. We kept the windows open in order to breathe the dust which coated our tongues. We parked at the plaza, a tree-filled spot semi-encircled by street and shops. Dark-skinned teen-age boys cruised and craned out of the windows of Chevies and Fords from the fifties. One of them yelled in a high nasal voice, "Americans, Americans!" We scuttled into the Hotel La Fonda, hoping he hadn't meant us.

My cousin was in Albuquerque and wouldn't be back until the following day, so we took a room in the cool hotel with its tile floors, Indian rugs, Mexican mirrors, and painted beds. We fell asleep to the buzz of flies, the hum of TV and of cars circling in the plaza. A few hours later we woke, hungry and curious about the town, but restaurants were closed and the plaza was nearly empty. Men in western hats and women in lacy bolero blouses sang and shouted in the hotel bar, but shutters were closed on the houses and the stars were silent in the sky. Streetlights were scarce. We went into a Seven-Eleven and bought stale cheese sandwiches, coke, potato chips, and a local paper. The young Mexican-looking woman behind the counter glared at us as though we had tried to steal something. We took our sandwiches back to the room and huddled in the glare of the TV because the lightbulb in the lamp was burned out.

I lay in bed and listened to the children breathe and wondered what kind of gall had brought us there. Who did I think we were? What arrogance had led me to believe that New Mexico would welcome us with flowers and fiesta? Whose land did I think it was? We had simply crossed another border, and we were too tired and too broke to go on. But I had made it into a movie in my mind—roots, flowers, and endless branches, grandchildren and great-grandchildren under cottonwood trees. So I consoled myself by saying, maybe it's just the letdown of having, at last, arrived.

Something crawled across my wrist. In order not to lie in bed and cry, I got up and went into the bathroom with the newspaper. I flipped past news of water shortage, petty crime, and local elections, until, on an inside page, a photograph struck me. It was a fuzzy picture of a strange structure, rising to a point at one end; it was called a chapel. The article said that Dr. Victor Westphall had built it himself in honor of his son who had died in 1968 in Vietnam. The monument was in a place called Eagle Nest, which I figured couldn't be too far away, because it was in the Taos paper.

At that time, August 1972, I was of two minds. One part was still taken up with the war. I couldn't fit together my old midwesternism and the CBS suppertime slaughter. I was dimly aware that the war had tied off certain veins. Old pleasures weren't as pleasurable. I read the newspaper instead of fiction, and I grew grumpy with small talk. I had beat my brains out being against things. I signed petitions against what was done in Southeast Asia in my name. My humor diminished and my cynicism flourished; after each new atrocity, I wondered, what will be the next one? The other part said, time to plant a garden and buy a horse; time to go without bagels, collective guilt, and Eric Sevareid. These deprivations will clear me with the sky and with the nighttime.

But bodies were still coming home in those water-proof, airtight, foamlined metal caskets. Today, ashes—or something—are coming back in coffins much too big for what they carry.

I tore the article out of the Taos paper and slipped it into my bag before I went back to bed.

Four

We stayed for awhile in a small house situated between the highway and the part of Taos Valley which belongs to the Indians. I woke each morning before sunrise, lay still in the coolness, dreading the onslaught of the sun. The Valley looked silvery, the pink and red hollyhocks which leaned against the screen were closed tight and wet with dew. Occasionally a scorpion ran the edge of the arched adobe fireplace. Not far from one window was a double-strand wire fence which signified the edge of Indian land. Their horses grazed there, and, out of sight, down a lane of cottonwood trees, lived the Pueblo. On the mountain behind was the Blue Lake, the sacred lake where Indians keep an eternal watch against intruders. Of course, white men fly over it in small airplanes and bring back reports.

A rich white woman in Taos paid the Indians $10,000 to

get into their sacred ceremonial structure, the kiva. Now she has seen it; what does she know?

Outside the other bedroom window lay the black highway with its lonely sounds: semis on their way to Texas; tourists beating the heat; local trucks lugging wood, hay, or piñon; house trailers; horse trailers. Once I woke in the dead of night and even then came the *whish whish* of passing tires.

As the sun oozed over the mountains, the flies attacked— face, arms, any uncovered flesh. I used to pull the sheet over my head and lie still, hoping they'd forget me, until their sawing drove me up and into the kitchen. Then, as I waited for the water to boil, staring out at the cloudless sky, the turkey vultures in the thin grass, I felt homesick for nowhere. Would it be better to be back on the road? Why were we there? We hadn't been able to find a place to live, so we were staying in a borrowed house. We were foreigners in a place we knew nothing about, surrounded by people we did not understand, by a history that was not our own. Maybe we had been seduced by stories of cheap labor, land, and ease, like everyone else. But we couldn't keep moving forever—this had to be as good as anywhere. I was stopped in my tracks, partly there, partly in the rest of the world. But New Mexico has a way of obliterating other landscapes, and the other world already seemed remote. Try as I might, I could not recreate a New England scene. I couldn't envisage the Lake where I had grown up, or West End Avenue in New York where I had lived for many years. Santa Fe, the capital of the state, has no airport. Sometimes I craved the sound of an airplane. But, still, they say you can put cash in a New Mexican's hand and take his land.

Mornings when my determination to stay there was at a low ebb, I hung out at Foster's Café because it is at the crossroads of town. One road leads to Santa Fe, one to Denver, the other to Raton.

One morning in September I paid my bill, stood in the dust outside Foster's with my heart pounding from coffee and excitement. I had dropped my children at their kindergarten where they played in a dusty courtyard and made God's eyes out of yarn.

The article about the chapel was crumpled in my bag; I got in the car and took the road to Raton. It wound up out of Taos Valley into cañon country: summer-sucked streams; aspens turning gold; bright orange cottonwoods looped by carnelian vines; log cabins set back in groves of spruce and pine. Occasionally the road ran off into a dirt path in a meadow which flowed uphill into the trees. I stopped at the top of the Palo Flechado Pass, 9,000 feet above sea level. My head hammered from the altitude and the exhilaration of the mountain land; I got out and walked around the car. Winter stirred somewhere in the pinegroves; I felt it was at my elbow.

Down, then, from the pass, around hairpin turns, straight out onto the road that enters the tan Moreno Valley. I saw it from several miles away—a small, white, pointed structure. As I drove, it grew larger. At the turnoff a faded green-and-white sign said: Vietnam Veterans Chapel. The ochre-colored dirt road wound up the hillside. The dry ground was covered with yellow camomile, sage, and purple Michaelmas daisies. Swallows crisscrossed in front of the car. Aspen and pine, like colored tears, ran down the sides of the Sangre de Cristo Mountains. Around behind the chapel was a weathered pick-up truck.

I got out and stood in the whipping wind. To the right of the chapel the cord of the bare flagpole beat against it, twanging. Suddenly, as if from nowhere, music began— Dylan singing "Blowin' in the Wind." I had a terrible desire to laugh. I felt I was on a film set—everything was unreal and topsy-turvy. The music made me think that someone was playing a trick on me. I shuddered, instead of laughing, and tried to pull myself together. I began to step down toward the large round steppingstones that led to the chapel door.

On either side of every stone, there were plain white markers:

Jerry Longtine	William Hamacher
Minnesota	New Jersey
Ray Williams	Clyde Hamby
Georgia	California

I stopped at each one until, finally, I couldn't look anymore.

A short, stooped man, deeply tanned and wearing sunglasses, came slowly around the corner. He nodded and motioned me to go inside.

While my eyes adjusted to the gloom, he stood in front of the row of photographs on the back wall. I stared at the cross which stood several huge steps down from where we were. Behind it a glass slit in the building gave a view of the valley and mountains beyond. The music followed us inside.

We sat down on the stone steps and talked. I told him that I had written a book about men who were wounded in the war. I wanted to understand how our country had become inundated by loss, and to know how a person like myself ought to behave. My father, who was his age, thought I was a subversive when I went on peace marches. He had been very angry with me during those past years, and, when I asked him why, he said, "The president has to be right. We have to have faith that he knows what he is doing." The president was Lyndon Baines Johnson.

The old man listened sympathetically, cocking his head as if he were somewhat hard of hearing.

"Most men my age," he said, "don't talk about Vietnam."

I wondered, self-pityingly, if I had been a son who had died in the war, would my father have built me a chapel? It was a childish thought, and I knew it. I still believed in pure expression and thought there was a place in the world for monuments.

The old man told me that David, his son, had died on May 22, 1968, and four months later, on September 10, he had dug the footings for the chapel. "I applied the last bit of stucco on September 10, 1972, four years to the day. I was not aware of the dates. I had just a little work left over the evening of the 9th, and so I finished on Sunday the 10th. There have been so many mysterious things about the chapel. For instance, I had concluded that there must be thirteen photos in the chapel, that the cross should be thirteen feet high, that we should fly the thirteen-star flag—the original Betsy Ross flag—a year and a half before I knew there had been thirteen men, including David, killed in the ambush at Con Thien. My birthday is October 13."

I wanted to get away, yet I wanted to say.

Outside we sat in the sun, near a plaque he had inscribed with one of David's poems.

If we are to
Stand on our feet in the
Presence of God, what, then,
Is one man that he should
Debase the dignity of
Another?

Who had debased his dignity, I wondered.

The old man pulled caramels out of his pocket and we ate them, watched a hawk dip down into the valley. I asked him how he had come to be there.

He squinted out across the valley towards the mountains that rose beyond the place called Angel Fire. "When I was a boy," he began, "it was like biblical times. I was born in Hebron, but we lived on a typical dairy farm near Fort Atkinson, Wisconsin. My great-grandfather came from Westphalia, in Germany. My grandfather came from the east; my grandmother, I think, from Canada. My father left the farm for a time during World War I, tried homesteading in Montana, but came back. My mother was from Illinois. There were three children—myself and two sisters. My father was a farmer and a carpenter in a factory.

"The farm was hard work. We had to get up at 4:00, and if we were through by 6:00 at night, we were lucky. All that has changed now. We are soft. I remember pulling water six miles on a stoneboat—like a wooden toboggan. Hand milling. We had twenty-one cows and it took time to get the milk. I walked to elementary school, one mile, a one-room schoolhouse."

I had been on farms in the Midwest, and I remembered bare floors, lumpy beds, and worn tables. People with thin faces and stern voices. Even though the milk comes out warm, it is not easy to milk a cow. People shiver in black winter mornings. The snow stays a long time, and spring comes grudgingly. The land is flat; the roads are menacing. When times are tough, jokes are rare, and music more rarely heard. Midwestern farmers are dour-skinned men.

"High school was six miles away. I wanted to play football, but, for a long time, Dad wouldn't permit it because I had to work on the farm. When I finally did get to go out, I had to skip half the practices. I got on the starting line senior year. At the evening practice after the first game, I broke my collar bone.

"I went to Milwaukee State Teachers College on and off for eight years because it was the Depression and I had to work. My first year I played on the starting line, broke my jaw, and had to have it wired together. It was real agony. Another season I ruptured my appendix. I didn't tell anyone, but it was so bad the only thing I could eat, finally, was oatmeal. It lasted six weeks. I played football for three of them, till at last I went to the county hospital. I had to be packed in ice for three days, to localize the infection, before they could operate. That was when I started losing my hair. I had to keep my job taking care of a crippled automobile salesman, carrying him everywhere.

"At one point I was working in a brewery. Because of the

dampness I got such bad arm cramps in practice that six teammates in relays rubbed out the cramps for three-quarters of an hour. Finally I had to have morphine.

"I wanted my sons to have every opportunity to do whatever they wanted to do in sports. And I always participated with them.

"When David was eleven months old, I would hold him overhead, standing in my hand. I'd drop him and catch him under his arms. He knew I wouldn't drop him.

"Even when he was little, David always wanted to compete. Once when I was in York, Pennsylvania, in the Navy, I went to a weight-lifting gym and he came along. I had forgotten his trunks. He wanted to work out, and I just couldn't understand his determination. It exasperated me. He started to cry until it turned out he could work out in his underwear.

"When we were stationed on the Atlantic coast he would go to the beach and let the waves toss him head over heels. He was absolutely fearless.

"David was an extraordinary physical specimen. In football he could beat another boy with a twenty-yard handicap. He made a touchdown the first time he carried the ball in high school. I nearly went crazy in the stand. It was the snob school of Albuquerque, too."

It had begun to rain in the sunshine so we went into the bunkerlike office which, in 1972, he was still building. We sat on rickety chairs near the glass door and it seemed we were balanced on the slope of the knoll. Sun came in and the room smelled of fresh pine. The old man's pipe had gone out while he was talking and he prodded and puffed it back to life. His hands were covered with swellings and nicks and bumps. It was as though he were on a mission, alone, in the cockpit of the chapel.

"Some of my peers look back on the Depression as horrible. I wouldn't trade it for the hassles young people have now—red tape, complications, wars, uncertainty. I have no sympathy for unwarranted nostagia or self-pity.

"I was in my senior year in college when I was married. My wife, Jeanne, worked in an ice cream store. We were married thirty-five years ago today."

I said that I would like to meet her and he looked surprised, then dubious. "I don't know if she'll see you, but I'll see what I can do."

I chalked it up to eccentricity, didn't say anything, and he went on.

"My destiny has always been with young people. After I graduated I was playgrounds recreational director for the city of Milwaukee. I volunteered for the directorship of the YMCA in Fort Dodge, Iowa. I was playing football in Fort Dodge, when I heard about Pearl Harbor. I was not for the military; in fact, I had quit a job in a factory that produced such things as electrical controls for submarines. But, when in Rome . . . you can't realistically divorce yourself from the world.

"Our country is good, the best in the world. I was born here and I don't know too much about other countries. It *is* the wellspring of freedom in the world, even though it has many failings. Unquestionably, the country has ways of doing things—military support, vicious and irresponsible things—still, you can't be in an ivory tower." He sighed,

"All my life has been a crusade to try to get down and make things different for myself and for other people. It's a fine line to draw.

"One hundred percent of the males in two generations of my family have volunteered their services to the military. All of us have looked upon military service and the defense of the country as one thing; being the bully on the block is another thing."

He spoke so glowingly that it took me a moment to sense the dichotomy between his familial pride and the fact that we were sitting beside a chapel he built to his son and other victims of our latest war.

"I volunteered for a three-year navy commission. I was trained for underwater detection, harbor defense, but I ended up establishing fleet post offices in the South Pacific.

"Jeanne, David, and Doug stayed with her family in Wisconsin. David was already quite a boy by then."

Later Jeanne showed me a little letter she kept in a shoe box, written on pink stationery:

> Dearest Daddy,
>
> Today we received our report cards, again I had satisfactory in all my subjects. Since school started I have gained 1½ inches in height and I weigh 45 pounds. A gain of 5 pounds. Don't you think I am really a big boy? . . .
>
> I will be glad when you come home Daddy angel.
>
> All my love
> David

He continued. "In the South Pacific I held the record for weight lifting. A dead lift of 603 pounds. It seems like everything in my life has been training me for this job on the chapel. It has been an enormous amount of work. I did the scaffolding, everything but the block laying, alone.

"I was in Balikpapan when the war ended. The afternoon it ended, Australian and Japanese soldiers, whose hatred for one another was legion, were bouncing along in the same jeeps together. I wondered why, now there is war, now we can be buddies?

"I wrote to Truman, saying how I felt about all this. I got a letter back from the War Department, more or less saying we'd just as soon you didn't write that kind of letter. I felt so alone, trying to create a democratic peace. I kept writing letters. People are apathetic, though. Nothing happens. I must be the only one, I thought, and maybe I'm a crackpot."

The trail from "biblical" Hebron, running past football and war, to the Blood of Christ Mountains, had indeed been a straight one. I wondered if, in some way, the chapel made up for David. It was, after all, less risky than a person.

"At times," he said, "David's death is still almost unbearable, at other times I can reflect on it with calmness. Sometimes it seems like the heaviest load a man can have to bear. But you come to grips with it. I know parents who can't talk about their dead boy. Some talk about him as if he were still here. That is my approach. I believe the chapel is a place of destiny. It stands for David's and other young men's philosophy—teach mankind to preserve instead of to destroy."

I didn't know if that had been David's philosophy. If it had been, why was he in the Marine Corps? But I decided that, for then, I had better take his word for it.

He waved at the chapel, as if he had made it like that—
with a gesture or with a wand. "I have a long way to get here
from our home in Springer, an hour and a half, to and fro.
I've put 40,000 miles on my truck on behalf of the chapel."
He paused, then went on, wincing. "After we sold the ranch
and moved to Springer, I made a schedule. I visited *all* the
churches, I gave 2,000 pounds of barbells to the school and
$1,500 worth of books to the library. There are 2,500 people
in the town and *nobody* came to see Jeanne. We were
unknown in Springer for a year. Now I talk with people
when I go to the post office, or to the store. They are ingrown
and clannish, even with their own people. Hardly anyone
from Eagle Nest—just up the road from here—ever comes
to the chapel. But, you know how a prophet is treated in his
own town."

I wanted to reach out, to put my hand on his arm, but I
suspected that he inhabited a place beyond fear, and beyond
mourning. He had a way of setting his chin and raising his
head, almost fiercely, as though he were hanging on, with
claws. He smoothed his forehead and his eyes began to tear
behind his dark glasses. "What about me," he whispered,
"day after day, the unbearableness of seeing his photo in the
chapel?"

We walked outside. The wind chilled my neck. Wheeler
Peak looked like it had snow on top, even though none had
fallen yet. I said, "Someone should write about it." He
stared at my eyes, as though he could drill something into
them. "It's part of destiny," he stated, "that a book be
written on the chapel."

Five

I drove away, turned at the last bend to see the old man watching my car. He looked like a stick figure beside the chapel, under an enormous sky. Although we had scarcely mentioned him, I thought that a book might be written about his son; but, even then, I sensed how difficult it would be to tip the balance in favor of the dead.

By October I had arranged to visit the old man's wife in Springer.

I drove past Foster's without a glance, took again the road to Raton, past chains of blood-red chilis drying beside adobe doorways, up out of Taos Valley. On a hillside, shadows of spruces ran parallel to the bones of an old house. New Mexico is full of startling shadows; they seldom come from people.

The Moreno Valley lay tan and yellow, beginning to fade

into sage gray. I passed the chapel—it seemed strange to know who was there and how it had come to be. The old man's pick-up truck looked like a toy. I passed the roads to Black Lake and Angel Fire. Passed the squat log cabins beside the lake which was cobalt-colored and tossed like the ocean. A piebald and a horse of many colors stood nose to nose in the sun. Clouds blew like breakers on top of Wheeler Peak. A bluebird flew over my car. Its color was extraordinary in the beige expanse.

I wanted to hear a woman's voice. I wanted to laugh. Even if it meant hearing about baby steps instead of football.

Higher, in Cimarron Canyon, red vines climbed through the golden aspen leaves, making runnels of enchanted light. My cousin had said, "It's New Mexico's graciousness, this Indian Summer." The road twisted along beside the green river beneath the Palisades—tan cliffs full of cracks and pale green and pink striations. They peered down at me. Huge rocks, Mayan shapes, and one that looked like a primitive hatchet, perched on top of them. I was running under the face of God. I had to stop the car and get out. The smell of resin was rich as food. The only sound was of the river and the wind in spruces.

Driving again, I stared hungrily at the few tents and campers beside the road. Part of New Mexico's mysteriousness is its emptiness. There are so few cars, so few people, that even if you want to, you cannot avoid the sound of the wind and the river. And that is a lonely sound.

Out of the canyon and out on the high plains I was glad to see the small places—Ute Park, Cimarron—with their solitary gas stations, bars, and cafés. Wood, for the most part, replaced adobe—west supplanting southwest. Out in the emptiness were Herefords, Black Angus, burros, a startled deer, a cattle dog, abandoned log buildings, ranches, and plains. A heart of something from long ago pounded as hard and fast as the horse that ran, tail and mane flying.

The mountains and mesas retreated, the land flattened: the shore of the Great Plains. I drove fast, past the hedgehogs and racoons that lay in their guts by the side of the road. Eventually there was an entire horizon without a rise, only wheat-colored fields, a windmill, abandoned shacks, cows, hay ricks and a Sunoco station between me and the sky. I thought about the old man driving this route every day, sixty miles each way, and about the exhaustion of it. The highway changed its number and I cut through dust swirled up by construction crews on the new superhighway that runs past Minnie's Dairy Delite and straight into Springer where no one would ever stop, except, if necessary, for gas.

I wanted to see the woman's side. I wanted to look at wedding pictures and talk about how hard it is to get along, about the heaviness of men and children.

Springer is trapped between two overpasses, one from the old highway, one from the new. It crouches in a semicircle of shade trees, shocking green foliage in a great bowl of earth colors. Even though the town is two-thirds Spanish, I might have been driving down the main drag of Jordan, Minnesota or Wall, South Dakota. It was all there: L&T Trailers, Ike's Court—One Mile, Car Wash Self Service,

Oasis Motel, Colfax Mills and Rangemaster Feeds, Schlitz, Café—Take–Out Order. The town seems to live in spite of itself, in spite of its having been passed by. There are signs, like lustrous patches of fur on an aging animal, that say it wasn't always that way: the Santa Fe Trail Museum—old brick, adorned with a gargantuan statue of a rifle–toting trapper—a faded green grade school, Nobles Department and Variety, Western Ways Indian Jewelry, Springer Turbine, the Glad Youth Center, Zia Movie House, Texaco greeting you with "Howdy Partner! Where Friend Meets Friend," Brown's Hotel advertising Steam Heat, a shutdown Republican Headquarters, Macaron's Sooper Market, the Cactus Club, abandoned but still wearing on its brick a jaunty top hat, gloves, and cane. People, mostly Anglos, cruised, slowed to honk hello to each other. I wondered if they had a sense of civic pride, if they had parades, a Chamber of Commerce; what did they do in winter; was there gossip, crime, pollution?

There were no answers in the buildings' faces or inside the cavernous Walgreen's where I sat at the soda fountain and ordered an Astronaut sandwich. Everything which life demands was provided there, even a dozen open wooden postboxes near the front door. And the pharmacist sat in his office at the back, watching a console model TV.

Did the people in the town purposely not go to see the old man's wife, or weren't they aware that she was there? What about the barbells and the books?

Plastered on the windows of the dingy barbershop, which flashed a neon "SNOOKER," posters boasted:

UNITED STATES
AIR FORCE
A CHALLENGE FOR THE BOLD

IT IS THE PEOPLE
THAT MAKE A GOOD JOB GREAT
WOMEN'S ARMY CORPS

THEN AS NOW
GUARDIANS OF FREEDOM
NAVY

THE MARINE CORPS
BUILDS MEN
BODY AND SPIRIT

I got back into the car, deciphered the directions the old
man had given me, turned right at the stop light.

I wanted to know how a woman survives the thing we still
never talk about, the thing that remains the definition of
pain: the death of our children.

I continued up the street, turned left, just before the old
bypass where a white frame house was for sale. Up a dirt
road, past a couple of houses which weren't for sale, there
was the white metal mobile home stuck in the strong sun,
behind a few spindling cottonwoods, beside an emerald-
colored putting green. A half-mile beyond, on a rise, the
Super Chief catapulted by, looking as though it were running right through the trailer, and racing on.

I went up a redwood step onto a small redwood stoop and
there she was. Small, like the old man, her eyes were sharp

and clear. She had an upturned, well-shaped nose and
pretty skin. She smiled at me, only a little shyly, and I shook
her hand, realizing I had wanted her to hug me. "Come in."
She opened the door and I stepped in.

"You'll have to excuse the mess." She gestured vaguely at
the slender living room which appeared fantastically tidy.
She sat in a large Naugahyde armchair and I sat, across from
her, on a long couchbed which was covered with a loose,
shiny blue spread. I was glad when she offered me some
coffee because, suddenly, I realized I was there to probe
obscenely into her life—tell me about your dead son, the
death of your son, the life of your dead son, the hopes and
dreams of a corpse which once came out of your womb.

We sat politely, somewhat stiffly opposite one another at
the linoleum-topped kitchen table where a plant curled a
red flower toward the sun kept at bay by white curtains. At
the edge of the table lay an odd lump, wrapped in a gaily
colored silk scarf. She noticed me looking at it. "I keep a
pistol," she spoke flatly, "there are so many funny people
around." By the way she spoke, I knew it was loaded.

I lost track of why I was there, forgot how I had planned to
begin. I tried to smile but the corner of my mouth twitched.
The kettle started to whistle and I nearly jumped out of my
chair. She got up to pour the coffee. The place hummed with
air-conditioning; it crept into my bones the way the dust
seeped in through the venetian blinds and the locked windows.

She stirred Coffee–Mate into my instant and I kept my
eye on her hand. I thought, I better get to the point so I can
leave. At the same time, of course, I was fascinated. I

managed to say that I guessed her husband had told her that
I was thinking of writing something about a soldier who had
died in Vietnam. It was what I had told him. She answered
by asking me the ages of my children. I said that they were
three and four and that that morning, before I left, my
daughter, Lila, had put her face close to mine and said, "I
see me in your eye," and then, referring to her brother who
was out of the room, "and I see Josh in the other eye."

She laughed, an infectious laugh, and her eyes crinkled at
the corners and looked very merry and blue. She shook her
head and said, "Kids!" I felt comfortable, suddenly; we were
on the ground I was seeking. I thought, so what if she has a
gun? She lives here in isolation. Just the same, I ate a
Hydrox cookie for comfort.

She told me that she had been reading David's letters for
the first time in five years that morning, and that she and the
old man had decided I was to see them. I understood that
she would have given it a great deal of thought, and I
suspected she would not have said this if I had been a man.

I asked how she kept her skin so pretty. New Mexico had
begun to suck at me and I saw dry lines under my eyes when
I woke in the morning. But hers was rich and clear, and
reminded me of women in the Midwest, women whose faces
said that they drank little, ate eggs, slept well, and rose
early. "Just that Ponds, you know . . ." She looked pleased,
but I hadn't meant to please her; I had really wanted to
know.

The trailer was long and narrow. I felt the way you do
when you are watching a film on a ship, or reading on a
train—still as you are, and unobservant of the outside, you

know that you are moving.

I told her that I wanted to ask her some questions and that I would probably write things down. She folded her small hands on the table. She spoke in the flat, unadorned manner of her part of the country:

"I was born in Highland, Iowa County, Wisconsin, a little mining town. I can see the street we lived on—it was sort of like Springer, had a big water tank, a lot of trees. Mother was French Canadian. Her mother was born in Wisconsin, but her father was born in Montreal.

"Father was Welsh and English, from Platteville, Wisconsin. He wandered over Iowa and North Dakota before he married. He was a barber. Everyone liked the way he did shaves and cuts. He always had asthma.

"I had three sisters and one brother. Mother had her hands full, housekeeping and baking. For thirty dollars a month we ate good—plenty of chicken and milk and butter. She canned and had her own garden. She never had a refrigerator until Victor and I bought her one after the war.

"She washed all the barber towels by hand because she was afraid of electricity and gas. She always put us in closets during storms.

"I don't remember needing anything in town. We used to pick berries, play on an old rock in the woods in the summer. In winter we went skating and tobogganing. Once when I was swimming I fell off a ledge and almost drowned. I was a tomboy. We made skis from barrel staves off old wooden barrels. We walked a mile back and forth to school and home for lunch—four miles a day.

"We went at various times to various churches. I have

never kidded myself that God doesn't know what I'm doing and saying."

I looked at her tan hands, her brown slacks and flower-print blouse, and I thought that whatever she had lost in the intervening years, she had retained a cleansweptness that is bred in small Wisconsin towns.

I said to myself, it is strange that God was spoken of here in the trailer, but wasn't mentioned at the chapel.

"After high school my sisters and I went to Milwaukee to find jobs. It was February, 1936, the Depression. We lived in rented rooms and couldn't find too much work. My first job was in an ice cream store, making double–dip cones. I made five dollars a week. I remember sometimes we ate bread and mustard but that wasn't very often. We didn't want to ask our parents for anything.

"When I first met Victor, I didn't want to go out with him. I wouldn't tell him where I lived so he followed me on the streetcar. Then he'd meet me on the corner, wait till the streetcar came. He worked evenings and I worked nine to eleven. He'd be sitting on the steps of the rooming house for me when I got home.

"We were married September '38 in Milwaukee—just friends, no relatives. We moved into a light housekeeping room with a little gas stove, a few cupboards, a wardrobe, and no closet. I worked till four months before David was born on January 30, 1940. When he was born, I said, ah, a GI. I just knew that was possible in his life.

"After Pearl Harbor Victor tried to get a commission but none was forthcoming. I was pregnant again. The day I brought Doug home from the hospital Victor's commission was in the mailbox. Whatever he did was all right as far as I was concerned.

"We sold all our things, got rid of our apartment, piled everything in the old Willys—even the washing machine—and drove, sometimes at night, to Viroqua, where my folks had moved. Doug was three weeks old. He caught cold and we thought it would be pneumonia."

I pictured them: Victor short and sturdy behind the thick old-fashioned wheel with its steering knob, Jeanne holding the crying, coughing baby—hot tiny hands—David wedged between diapers and cartons in the back, blowing and then drawing a face on the frosted window, feet cold, imagination devoid of their destination. Hour after hour the squalling, the thin dark road piled high on either side with sculptured snowbanks. The car, the clothes, the songs they sang were different from the ones I know, but the road was the same.

The boy in the back seat got used to moving—"we've moved forty-two times since we were married," Jeanne said. I looked at his mother who outlived him. Her life mapped out my duality. We make homes and then we prepare ourselves and our children to leave them. American women have always done it; it was the law of the frontier and we live in its aftermath.

I felt that crossing borders was something I and my children had to be able to do. Stories about my ancestors gleam in my head and I especially love the one about the young couple who reached the Mississippi, agreed to take the first boat that came along, and to settle where it took them. It took them to Minnesota, and there they spent their lives.

Wherever I go, I make a home with the ferocity of a nesting bird; and all the while I am wondering what the next step will be. Our ancestors moved mostly because they had to; I don't know why I do it.

American women developed, by necessity, the toughness that European women sense in us. I looked at the old woman's sweet face, her workmanlike hands, and I saw, in both of us, splits as deep as rivers. Old Women, New Women, we sit in our kitchens, listening for sounds, waiting for signs of leaving.

"I stayed with my folks and Victor went into basic training. In April, I loaded the boys into the car, stayed in motels with mice running around in them, and drove out to join him. Everyone thought I was nuts. In Princeton, New Jersey, we stayed in one room with a hot plate and a double electric grill for about three months. Then we went to Fishers Island, stayed in the summer cottage of a big mansion with four or five other families. They ruined the house.

"From there we went to Rehobeth Beach, had a nice cottage with another family, but the woman and I were at each other's throats. Sharing washdays and everything just didn't work out.

"For Victor's leave we drove back to Wisconsin. He left at the end of December '42.

"The town seemed not too lively to me so I went to the hardware store and got me and David skis and sleds with metal runners. My father was a newspaper nut and took the Milwaukee papers, so we read lots of them. I took care of the children, wrote letters, and listened to the news. Victor was in the Pacific, my brother was in Europe.

"David used to stand for hours looking at books and magazines. I used to read to him a lot. When he went to school, he was reading. When he was in first grade, they told me he was reading at eighth grade level. He got into a lot of scraps on the school ground. I can't remember so much about Doug.

"David was a fearless child. Once he was almost killed by a car crossing the street. When he was real tiny and I took him to the store with me, he would run away, so he had a harness like a little doggie on a leash. I never needed it for Doug; he used to cling to my skirts.

"David was always picking flowers. He used to help in my mother's garden and he'd talk to all the neighbors. One lady said it was just like talking to a grownup.

"Once he came home with the scrawniest, ugliest kitty and I wouldn't let him keep her. I wonder if he thinks I'm terrible for that.

"In the summer we went to stay with Victor's family. They had a big old house. His mother died while he was overseas. She was only fifty-two. She had all white hair by the time she was thirty. She got pneumonia because the house was so cold. Victor was coming from San Francisco to Chicago, then on by bus, but the bus didn't stop in the town so I had to go to the nearest town where it did stop.

"I took the children, and got two hotel rooms. The bus was supposed to come at 10:00, but it didn't and the hotel desk was closed. I kept going to the phone and calling Victor's father and waking him up. He must have thought I was nuts. Victor arrived at 2:30 A.M. David remembered him."

A parent remembers such events with love and sentimentality. A child remembers the dark, strange sounds and smells, a bulging bed, a different kind of mother. The idyll ends; the race begins.

Peacetime brought home a million wars.

"Victor tried to stay in the Navy but he was three years over the age limit.

"I had been sick with asthma and chest pains, but had postponed going to the doctor. Finally, when I went, he said I had TB and should go to New Mexico. Even though I had paid my folks rent and shared on food while I was living with them, I tried not to spend over $125 per month, and we had saved $3000 from Navy pay. We bought a house trailer, second-hand, in Milwaukee.

"Victor kept a diary."

"February 1946. We left Milwaukee at noon . . . starter wouldn't work so we bought a new battery but it did no good. . . . Springfield, Illinois . . . snow on the ground in the morning . . . a sailor tried to pass us on a hill and, after passing the trailer, pulled over too soon and collided broadside with our car. Our little car was doing fine on the Ozark Hills. Everyone wonders how it does it. A twenty-five foot, 5000 lb. trailer looks awfully large behind a Willys coupe . . . blowout on the right hand trailer tire at Joplin, Missouri . . . flat tire on the car where the fender had scraped it when the sailor ran into us. . . . slept alongside the road at intervals that night. (Jeannie says, who slept?) . . . stopped at Claremore, Oklahoma for gas and noticed that the new tire on the right hand side of the trailer was going flat . . .

slept for a time near Tulsa, Oklahoma. . . . 12:00 that night another flat on the trailer while we were passing thru Oklahoma City . . . blew out the right hand tire . . . reliner put in an old 4-ply retread and left about five pm . . . three miles and that tire blew out . . . broke an axle trying to get the trailer off the highway and went to bed . . . Amarillo, Texas about 5:00 A.M. . . . flat on the left hand trailer tire . . . reaching high altitudes and were stuck on a couple of hills and had to be helped up . . . first time a couple of sailors and second time a local rancher . . . arrived at Santa Rosa, New Mexico . . . stuck on Santa Rosa Hill about four miles out . . . fuel pump was not putting out for such high altitudes . . . a fellow helped us over Palmo Hill so don't know if we could have made it or not . . . one more flat tire near Clines Corner and then drove on to Moriarty . . . thought it might snow so were tempted to try the last big hill . . . decided not to and stopped for the night 26 miles from Albuquerque . . . left the trailer behind and went on into Albuquerque to look it over . . . all the trailer parks are bursting at the seams . . . wasn't any room anywhere for our trailer . . . fearful of the one big hill so had a fellow in a huge cattle truck help us to the top . . . very slowly and we were able to put slack in the chain . . . so we knew we could have made it by ourselves . . . Hilltop Cafe—elevation 7300 feet . . . dropped 2100 feet into Albuquerque . . . drove on to our brand new lot over a very bumpy road and arrived just at dusk . . . decided it would be a good investment to build a house on our lot and then went to bed. Postlude: We like Albuquerque very much. New Mexico ably lives up to its slogan 'The Land of Enchantment.'

P.S. We are going to build that house. I have started my classes at the University. I am taking a graduate major in History and a divided minor in English, art education and Philosophy. This all leads up to a Ph.D. in American Civilization."

"Albuquerque was only 35,000 people then but there was a tremendous housing shortage. Our lot was on the west side, across the Rio Grande, near the University. The lot cost $500. There was nothing but us, the trailer, and the mountains, the desert, and a few cottonwoods. We had a washtub outside. There were candle moths and an irrigation ditch where we found calves that had fallen in. I was always afraid the children would fall in.

"At first I was frightened by the mountains. I used to think, what am I doing here?"

I wanted to ask how long it took her to get used to them because I was scared of those mountains, too, and every day I looked at them and wondered what I was doing there. People in Taos said the high ion count caused our severe depressions. The children were often sick with high fevers that came in the night. Our dog was hit out on the highway and would limp forever. The Indians hid scornful faces from us; the Spanish looked at us as though we had murdered their mothers. But, most of all, in the face of its indescribable beauty, the land seemed to threaten us, to forbid us further access. Stick to your seamy little town, the streams seemed to say; stay, the mountains seemed to growl. So we took picnics up in them and came home before nightfall. We drove; we didn't even know how to begin to make the pact that some people had made with that land in order to travel on it by foot.

D. H. Lawrence, who was supposed to love the place, wrote about the harshness of the earth, the destruction of the people, the "malevolence" of the mountains.

Wondering how she had managed to lose her fear, I realized that fears merely replace one another. We only imagine that they disappear in the roundabout of weekdays and weekends, the whitewash of childbearing years; later, in quieter times, we see that they are still there, perhaps only in different guises.

The mountains are far away from Springer.

"Victor went to school and I got a job at the Sandia Base checking trays in the cafeteria. David was in school, but Doug was only three and he had to stay home alone. He was good, but sometimes he'd lock himself out and he couldn't get lunch and I'd come home and he'd be crying. I used to worry about him all day.

"After school and work we built a garage and moved into it. David didn't like living in the garage because the other children teased him. Then we started a house. Victor built it, the boys and I helped. It was cement block with a wood beam ceiling, concrete floor with asphalt tile.

"Victor had never done any of this before, but he can do whatever he sets his mind on.

"Even when David was tiny he had to help his father in the building business. In the summer Victor made them work mornings and have some athletics afternoons. David didn't like the regimentation and he resented it. The same as

Victor and his father—the same as Victor resented the work
on the farm. David told me of his resentment but he never
told his father.

"I never remember Victor kissing the boys."

I had a sinking feeling. If he had lived to have a son, would
David have kissed him? In our time of prescribed touching,
perhaps we make too much of kissing, but I don't think so.
And, surely, picking up a baby, letting him fall and catching
him under the arms, is no substitute for hugging. Had
Jeanne been disappointed in Victor as a father, or was it all
part of a tradition she understood? I didn't know how to ask
her.

"Everyone was building and there was a shortage of building material. There was no floor tile in Albuquerque so we
went back to Wisconsin and bought a tow trailer, bought
floor tile for the bathroom. We had to go to several lumber
yards to get even a pound of nails. We laid tile, and did all
the painting. We did everything ourselves. The house cost
$3000 and we sold it for $6000.

"In '49 we bought two lots, built a duplex next door,
mostly all by ourselves. Victor would get up early to work
because he was going to school all the time. We built a
triplex, rented two units and lived in the other. Then we
sold it. Victor doesn't stop. You wear out, but he doesn't
realize that.

"The year we were in the triplex a car hit David and threw
him on the hood. He also had a cyst in his neck. The doctor
said the biopsy showed it was cancerous and he had to have
X-ray treatment. The same doctor said his tonsils were bad

and he also hadn't been circumcised, so they did it all at the same time. It took five nurses to hold him down when he came to.

"Nothing special ever happened to Doug.

"Once they were playing in the bunk beds with some other kids. One of them shot David in the nose with a BB gun; it got infected and he had to have the BB taken out. Then his nose had to be lanced because the doctor said the infection was going to his brain."

She raised her hands and let them fall with a helpless gesture. It's a terrible joke: you care for a child, take him to doctors, dentists, and kindergarten, nurse and comfort him, sing and read to him, play with him, tell him fibs and give him toys; you coddle him, and kiss him, and listen for him in the morning. One day you realize his feet are bigger than yours and soon he can see the top of your head. You see a young man and you remember him in his crib; you don't mention it because you don't want to embarrass him in his rush to manhood. He marries; you watch wistfully. He studies and works and earns money. He goes off to war; you remember the first time he walked. Then he dies.

Indians of the Amazon have a legend that tells of mothers following their dead children into the grave.

"I quit my job and Victor bought more lots. Albuquerque was booming; it was the big distribution point for the state. There was the railroad, the air force and nuclear bases, the University. We were crazy. We made money to start and it all began with the $3000. We earned it! Nobody else on my side of the family ever had $3000 in the bank. Victor bought five lots and hired two guys, worked night and morning, got an FHA loan, formed a partnership with a fellow from Chicago named Davis, and went into building in a big way. We bought lots for $100 apiece; when we quit in '62 they were $4600 apiece. The first houses were $5450 for one bedroom, $5850 for two. We built 300 houses before we quit."

It occurred to me that not only had she never cherished the money they earned, but that she came from a place where people harbor a profound mistrust of the rich, where money is associated with crookedness or with indolence. I suspected that she was happier with the life they had now. I had a hunch that if I shook out a satchel and dumped a million gold pieces at her feet, she would stare at them, unmoved. I was hard put to imagine what would impress her.

"Mostly, though, we just went on every day. We had clubs, like the Lions, the PTA, church—ours was the First Congregational—and the kids brought home their report cards. Sometimes, in summer, we'd go up to Red River, which is near Eagle Nest, and we'd sleep in the Nash. We had food and an icebox. I'd stay at the car with the possessions and Victor and the boys would hike. Red River only had three motels then. It was pretty and quiet and cold in the mornings.

"You go on and you don't realize what's happening.

"One time we had been camping at Bandelier when Victor began to feel ill. Then one morning he couldn't get out of bed, started turning purple from his liver not working. He was in bed for weeks with Wile's disease—he lost forty pounds. The doctor said, 'You'll never lift weights again,' but he persisted, even though he was so weak he had to sit on a metal stool in the shower and fell, once, getting out. While Victor was sick, David had a bike accident and broke his arm. At the hospital I went into the operating room, saw they had put him to sleep and hadn't even strapped him on. I had to grab him and strap him and he started to regurgitate so they must have fed him.

"While Victor was ill, we bought eighty acres on the west face of the Sandia Mountains, east of Albuquerque. Later he said he wasn't in his right mind when he bought it, but he was determined to build there. We thought it would cost $24,000; it turned out to be $48,000. The boys harped at us for having a big home and two cars.

"The house had a flat roof, an awning, a two-story living room. We lived there from '52 to '61. We were up there all alone. I was afraid of being on the mountain alone. Once the police came up and said they had heard there was a body nearby."

In the house I finally rented outside Taos we slept on mattresses on the floor in front of the fireplace. Sometimes, when the fire had gone down to a glow, I woke to the howl of coyotes. The sound made me think of a corpse crying. I understood how the teeth of fear had eaten into her in the house on the side of the Sandia Mountains.

"We had to drive the boys back and forth to school. A few times Victor forgot to pick David up. We were isolated and there were no friends for the boys.

"We went out of that business and had our own business. I kept the books. We had an office in a model home, built 180 houses. We had options on other land, but finally we said

nuts to this business, bought a block on the east side of
Albuquerque, built sixteen apartments in 1959. We built
twenty more in '62 and sold the other half of the block. It was
a rat race."

The trailer hummed. We huddled, flanked by the matching avocado-colored stove and refrigerator. A chill had
seeped into my bones, as though I had been sitting still in
the autumn shade for a long time. I shivered from the
relentless stream of air-conditioning from vents on the floor,
even in the middle of the wall–to–wall carpet. I went to the
bathroom and when I came back, she had brought out an old
briefcase, a shoe box, and a Whitman Sampler box stuffed
with David's papers. She rifled through official letters,
credit card letters, bonds, old bills. She showed me photographs of members of the family—preserved events, cap-
tured faces. There was one of herself, Victor, and the boys
standing beside the old Willys and their first trailer—strong,
young people, feet planted firmly, well-grounded people.
People with hope, a plan, a future. I examined the face of the
oldest boy, and saw nothing but childlike eagerness.

"He was a beautiful boy," I said.

She ironed the photo with her palm. "He's in grave #510
at the Santa Fe Military Cemetery. He used to march up and
down with a flag during the war while his father was away. I
wanted to tape a flag to his tombstone but they don't allow
anything on the graves."

She pulled out his birth certificate, certificate of baptism,
report cards. "I don't have to like any of it, but it's here." She
handed me documents pertaining to an official military
death: belongings, remains, burial. Bold printed words, and

smaller ones, heavy lines and thinner ones, blocked–off
spaces, boxes for checks, abbreviations and numbers,
scrawled signatures, all filed beneath my eyes:

REPORT OF CASUALTY 2947–68 FINAL J H/gfc
29 May 68

WESTPHALL   Victor David III

1877202
plp23ip/p3p2 1st Lt usmc
4th MAR DIV (REIN) FMF FDO SFRAN 96602
co B 1st BN

X   B   non–battle KIA

Died 22 May Quang Tri Province (   ) Republic of
Vietnam result gunshot wound to the body from
hostile rifle fire while engaged in action
against hostile forces.

Interested persons   Footnotes
Mr Victor W Westphall Eagle Nest N Mex Fath
                         87718
Mrs Jeanne Westphall   "   Moth
Walter D Westphall   "   Bro

CERTIFICATE OF DEATH

From (Ship or Station)

BRAVO COMPANY, 1st BATTALION, 4TH MARINES

5. Length of service
   7 yrs 9 mo

12. Date of birth	13. Age	14. Religion
January 30, 1940	28 yrs 4 mo	Unitarian

15. Color of eyes	16. Color of hair	17. Complexion
Brown	Brown	Fair

18. Height	19. Weight
69"	175 lbs

20. Marks and scars (noted in health record)
    Scar (L) knee 1.5 cm
    No others noted in health record

30. Summary of facts relating to death:
    While in an active duty status with the 1st
    Battalion, 4th Marines, participating in
    Operation Kentucky in the vicinity of Con
    Thien, Republic Vietnam, 1st LT WESTPHALL
    sustained W/M penetrating the back and upper
    and lower extremities.

Death was instantaneous.
Identification was made by fellow Marines.
No autopsy was performed.

---

31. Disposition of remains:
    Remains of the deceased transferred to the Danang
    Mortuary for further transfer to the Continental
    United States for further disposition.

I felt dry-mouthed, as though I were in a traffic jam, creeping toward the scene of an accident. I wondered what it had been like for the person who sat, day after day, typing up those forms. I looked at the woman designated as "Moth." "I wonder," I said, "how you bear it."

"It's five years since his death. It doesn't get any easier. People say, forget about it, but you just bear it all alone. It's not only me; it's all the rest of them. Some of them carry the telegrams they received about their son's death around with them. I've seen them at the chapel—they're broken into shreds."

"I think of my little boy dying and I can't imagine what I would do. What can a person do?"

She seemed not to have heard me.

"I went to the chapel all last summer and I can't go back. I don't trust the people around there."

She seemed to be slipping away from me. "It might have been easier for us without the chapel. Even before David's body came, we thought of a chapel. I thought of scholarships. Then I thought of a Peace and Brotherhood Chapel—something small and quiet. I also thought of giving some of the money to a niece and nephew for college. But I didn't talk about that because, by then, Victor and Doug wanted the chapel. I wanted to wait and not spend the money. Victor said it was my idea.

"David had $30,000 insurance money. We told the architect we had $20,000 and would have let Doug have the other ten. While I was away in Albuquerque, the architect drew up a $30,000 plan.

"Now I don't go to the chapel because I'm too outspoken. I say what I think to people.

"It scares me to death Victor going over there all the time. Who knows who might have it in for him? They could stop him on the highway, and, then, he's usually up there all alone. Every day I just wait for him to come back."

The kitchen sink made a sound as though it were clearing its throat. She glanced around at it. "Even the plumbing is an informer."

I laughed, happy that her humor had returned. But she leaned toward me, gripping the edge of the table, stricken. She got up and hurried toward the door. "When David was in the hospital after he'd been bitten by a snake, there was a Vietnamese girl on the ward who was dying of malnutrition. The guys called her Twiggy. David was shocked. After he died, some time after we moved here, there were some guys hanging around—something to do with Victor. One of them kept holding some twigs; he just kept on holding them and feeling them. I know he got his hands on that letter from David. So now I try to never leave these things."

She pulled aside the venetian blind from the door window, showed me how easy it would be to remove the whole window and get in. I had to agree that it would not be hard.

I wondered who would want to, though; I tried to follow her out onto her battlefield. I saw her, a sentinel at the redwood stoop, guarding a home that was a tomb for a known soldier. I believed that she took her duty as seriously as any grunt on patrol at the darkest jungle hour. But, try as I might, I could not sight the enemy.

Six

Her enemy could have been in the mountains, on the winding roads, or in the past. It could have been isolation, imagination or the decay of that corpse in grave # 510 in Santa Fe—the child who marched with a flag turned to a common heap of grown–up bones.

Surely our enemies were different. Mine was the sense of disorientation I lived with that year. I missed the stench of New York City, the glib intelligence, the rude self-assurance of easterners. At night we heard the coyotes. Day after day we woke to the mountains.

In northern New Mexico you measure where and how you are by the mountains. You're either up to them, or you aren't. They make rivers seem sluggish, the desert inert. People live under them, on them, at their feet, on their rims, in their shadows. There is an unending dialogue between them. Men barter with them, for time. And they only stand there, silent as gravestones.

Death encumbered the land. It lurked in the flash floods which swept away cars, animals, and houses. It leered out of the Penitentes' crude wooden deathcarts. It stank in the rotting corpses of Indian horses; it cried in the whine of the flies; it wheeled with the turkey vultures and encircled the valley on hawk wings. It hee-hawed in the face of the Mongoloid child who used to come to my door. It lined the hands of Georgia O'Keeffe who was learning, blindly, to wrap them around clay pots in her ninetieth year of defiance. It buzzed in the high tension wires that stretched down from Four Corners. It hung with the crutches and canes that plastered the wall of the church at Chimayo—offers of thanks for miraculous cures. It ringed the graveyards. It pointed frantic fingers at sorcerers in a region where the second religion is witchcraft, where forced confessions and hangings are tradition. It sulked in the hatreds of one for the other in Taos—mean in a mean town. It fingered me at the nape of my neck when I walked Spanish roads, and the dog at each house took up the barking of the last.

Sometimes I felt that if I could live through living there I could live through anything. I told myself that I would be all right because I was cosmopolitan and uprooted, but I wasn't all right, because I didn't know what I needed to make me feel at home. I met homesick Anglos everywhere, some of them resigned, others seeking out places that reminded them of their youth, fighting the obliteration of the past that comes with the staggering landscape. I felt like a fly stuck on the territory.

We went to ceremonies and celebrations, hungry for the solace of community, for the saving grace of ritual. In the autumn we went to San Geronimo Day at the Pueblo, which is tucked under the mountain's chin. Indians brought silver, turquoise, food, dolls, belts, and beads for Anglos to buy. The evening before, people milled around the large space in front of the old adobe buildings with their doors painted apple green or French blue, their round mud chimneys, their vigas and ladders. The houses seemed quieter and more forbidden than ever. Skinny dogs fornicated beside the thin, littered stream. Indians set up stands, pulled goods out of their campers, cooked meat over small fires. It looked like a campground in an ancient setting. We bought pepper sausage sandwiches that seared our mouths, and fled.

The next day we joined hundreds of other cars that crept back up the dusty lane lined with glistening cottonwoods. At the center of the pueblo a slaughtered lamb hung upside-down from the top of a high wooden pole. Vendors' hot eyes followed us as we walked from stand to stand. After awhile people started murmuring, "Here come the clowns, the clowns." Six men with black painted bodies, wearing corn sheaves for loin cloths, jumped off the buildings and snaked through the crowds. We lost sight of them until, suddenly, they reappeared, running straight at us. The leader bent down to my daughter, opened his mouth, and screamed in her face. He moved on, and the next in line leaned toward her, while I, feeling fettered by slow motion, picked her up and held her like a baby. The other clowns wove around behind us, yelled at her, and ran on. I sat down in the dust, gripping her, and slowly grew aware of her screaming.

The Indians who stood around us laughed at us. The lamb hung in the sweltering sun.

I interpreted it, of course, as racism. I thought about packing up and moving on—it would have been as good an excuse as any. Several days later someone explained to me that the clowns are the Indians' equivalent of Santa Claus. Indians tell their children that if they are naughty, the parents won't give gifts to the clowns, and the clowns will take the children away. During San Geronimo, the clowns, who had been eating peyote for several days beforehand, can do anything they like. They throw people in the stream, run through the throng, and scare whomever they please. Being scared is supposed to be an honor. Even so, it was a long time before we went back to the Pueblo.

I noticed that only Anglos who had been in New Mexico a long time had warm connections with the Spanish. It is difficult for us to fathom the Spanish-Americans' secret, stubborn ways, so we whisper about them, particularly about a group of them called the Penitentes, or the Brothers of Light.

In the sixteenth century, Franciscan friars belonging to a penitential order came with the Spanish conquistadores to northern New Mexico. They converted Pueblo Indians who had lived in the area for 15,000 years; they kept up the faith among the Spanish, and their order, whose laws included flagellation, spread across the isolated mountain area. After the Mexican revolution in the early nineteenth century, all Spanish-born Franciscans were sent out of the country. Laymen were left to take over church practices in the small villages where, eventually, every non-Indian New Mexican

was Catholic and Penitente. Because of their excessive practices, the Archbishop in Santa Fe sent warnings and signs of
disapproval and forbade the Brothers of the Light to celebrate mass in their chapels which are called moradas. In
spite of the church's position, the practices of the Penitentes
flourished well into the twentieth century.

One of the few outsiders ever to see and record the
Penitentes' rites was a newspaper reporter from Denver, D.
J. Flynn, who, in 1894, went to Taos on an assignment from
Harper's Weekly, to see their Holy Week rituals. In the
procession one man carried the crucifix, another played an
eerie dissonant tune on a pito, or reed flute. Chanters
followed, and behind them came two flagellants wearing
white pants and black bags on their heads. Their backs had
been sliced with glass or flint pieces and they walked
barefoot over thorns and cacti. They flagellated their own
backs so brutally that they could barely pull the cactus whips
out of their skin. They gave themselves at least 500 lashes
before they got to the crucifix. "So sharp and knifelike were
the whips that the entire covering of flesh had been torn off,
leaving the bones of the ribs exposed to full view."

After this group went into the morada, more men appeared. Two masked men each carried crosses weighing
around 400 pounds and two other men whipped their naked
backs. Others came behind, also whipping, and, finally,
others came carrying figures of saints.

That evening Flynn had the opportunity to see one of the
flagellants.

"I cannot describe the condition of his back, but it looked
as though sharp knives had been drawn across it in all

directions and the flesh torn out with pincers."

The following day Flynn saw the Penitentes' enactment of the crucifixion with a wooden figure tied to the cross. At other times, however, they have been known to fasten a man to the cross with ropes or wet buckskin thongs. Some reports contend that men have been nailed to the crosses.

With time, better roads, education, and a greater number of priests, the Penitente practices have softened. But it was not until 1947 that they were accepted back into the good graces of the church, and, even then, it was with the admonishment that "the Brethren proceed with moderation and privately under our supervision." Today the man in the field, in the market, almost anyone in northern New Mexico could be a Penitente. Anglos speculate about them, stare suspiciously at the moradas and wonder about their Easter processions from which they are still barred.

When my cousin lived in Talpa, a small Spanish community outside Taos, the Penitentes came and asked her to keep her curtains drawn during the time of their procession. She obeyed, feeling like a stranger in her home.

In a place where Indians and Spanish live by secrets and by tradition, an Anglo feels lonely at the movies, sad at the Seven-Eleven, forlorn in front of his Christmas stocking.

Not long after we settled there, I heard an Anglo woman say, "I used to feel bad about the Chicanos, but now I don't give a shit. They look at you like they'd like to rip your guts out." I saw those looks and I got them. But I also heard transported Californians complaining that they were not allowed to have swimming pools because of the water shortage. And I met a midwestern architect who bought land up in a canyon, and who, in a drought-ridden land, used water there to curry his golf course.

Hatreds translated themselves into a stream of daily incidents. The son of a beloved Anglo doctor in Taos was training for the Olympics. He had to stop jogging along the highway because so many Spanish people tried to run him down. A friend came to visit us and we put him up in a studio we had rented in town. One night he went to a Spanish bar which he didn't realize was off limits for Anglos. He had a beer and went back to the studio. In the middle of the night, the police—who are nearly all Spanish—pounded on the door, demanded to know who he was, whose studio it was, and other questions which amounted to a warning. Another friend was driving home on a winter night when his car broke down. He walked to the nearest house and asked if he could use the telephone. The Spanish man wouldn't let him in, but said that he would call for him. In a few moments the police arrived, grabbed him, forced him into their car, beat him up, and threw him in jail.

We went to a Democratic picnic out in a field the year the country elected Richard Nixon. It was hot and dusty in the field, but there was a lot of food. The speeches were all in Spanish and we sat for awhile, listening to them. No one was rude to us, but no one spoke to us either.

Winter came down like a hatchet. Indoors, in the piñon smoke, flies continued to breed. Magpies flew against my window, and at dusk, dogs barked all over the town.

At that time in Taos eighty percent of the people had no indoor plumbing. I used to feel embarrassed and mean when I saw women washing their clothes out-of-doors, pulling clumps of dripping sheets out of vats, steaming in the icy air. Then our well ran dry. We carried water in garbage cans from my cousin's house. We carried it across the field where the cows stood like snow-dusted statues, and on up the steep hill. We shat in plastic bags and used snow to wash our dishes. I thought about water all the time—about rivers, streams, rivulets, tributaries, ponds, lakes, oceans, springs, and sewers. Our clothes grew crusty and our tempers short.

Our nearest neighbor was an old Spanish woman who lived in a hut with her middle-aged, retarded son. Her other son, who ran a welding shop, lived in a house on the other side of her. A great many cars made their way up his rutted road and Anglos whispered that he was a leader in the militant Spanish-American organization called La Raza. He was elegant and handsome and spoke perfect English. Sometimes I saw him at sunset, standing outside his home, gazing across the valley at the mountains.

The well man, an Anglo who wore a western hat and spat through his teeth continually, came to look at our well, pronounced it hopeless, at least until spring. He said that the welder had a well and had never given his mother water, but that the year before she had received a government subsidy and so now had her own. He suggested that we ask her for water. One afternoon I went to see her.

She and her son lived in one room—two beds with metal frames, a table with an oilcloth cover, two chairs, a fireplace, a crucifix, and a Richard Nixon calendar. We talked the way women do when they speak each other's language badly. We said that my children were beautiful, that the weather was cold, and that life was hard. She said that she would be glad to give us water. After that, we used to go to her well in the afternoons, and she would come to the door and beam at us, tell us that it would not be long until spring, the streams were beginning to flow. It was our only Spanish connection. I used to look forward to seeing her. As much as I remember the town, I remember her, especially how, in places, her teeth were missing, giving her a crooked and wonderful smile.

We visited a religious commune, called Lama, which was founded by Baba Ram Das, who, when he was a professor at Harvard, used to be Richard Alpert. In the sixties counter-culture people invaded northern New Mexico. They set up communes in the hills, in the desert, in old adobe houses in the town. In warm weather, at the hot springs, they spread out their shawls, their biodegradable soaps, and their baggies full of homegrown. They lay naked in the hot water and on the banks of the springs. Spanish boys, whose closest contact with female nudity was the magazine rack at the Seven-Eleven, came to gawk, dropped their beer cans, and brandished their knives. The flowerchildren fought back—two cultures hacking it out by waters that are older than the Indians remember. News of these battles spread through the Pueblo, and the old men shook their heads, listening to the whispers of their mountain.

At Lama there is no drinking, smoking, or drugs. Members of the commune build their houses, grow organic vegetables year round, run their own school. We went on a Sunday, the day visitors are allowed. We drove up through snow which inched down the mountainside, through light blue hazes and mists and severe green shadows shot down-

hill by gigantic pines. It looked as though the entire
Southwest was spread out below—dark blue mesas and
mountains, sere valleys and plains on either side of the gash
made by the Rio Grande gorge. We passed the school building, a swing on a tree, and went up to the adobe house with
its large communal tile tub, plants, and devastating view.
Small houses made from freshly cut pine were secluded one
from the other and were simple and pretty.

While we were walking around, a young man passed us,
nearly staggering under a load of lumber. He was trying to
climb over a fence and I offered him a hand. He looked at me
gratefully, pressed his fingers to his mouth, and shook his
head. I thought that he was a mute, but later learned that he
was observing a religious silence.

The prayer meeting took place in a whitewashed adobe
room with sheepskin rugs placed all around; two steps led
down to an altar with some cups and a burning candle. We
sat cross-legged on the rugs and chanted. I got cold and stiff,
but after awhile my hands grew warm and began to tingle.
The rest of me was neither lost nor placed. I was connected
to what was happening in the room, but also, to something in
the universe. I don't know how long we stayed there. After
awhile people began to get up, bow, and back out the door. I
left, too, without a bow. I wasn't sure what I would have
been bowing to.

After a lunch of macrobiotic soup, health bread, and
apples, we gathered in the main building for Sufi dancing. A
woman beat the drum. "Take off your shoes and move
clockwise." Around and around, grown-ups and children,
some in long skirts, some in yoga pants, the guests in mun-

dane outsiders' clothes. The drum repeated and we followed the steps.

At sunset we walked back to the car. "Would you like to live in a place like that?" I asked the children. "Yeaaaaaah," they squealed. I gazed at their flushed faces and I felt jealous of them. They required so little to feel that they belonged.

We visited the state citadel of Angloism—Los Alamos, where they still dig up Indian relics and put them on display in the atomic museum. The guide spoke charmingly about fission and fusion, urged us to push the buttons on science exhibits, and led us past Little Boy and Fat Man, old nuclear bombs sitting in a tidy courtyard.

The town has an abundance of churches. The old wooden building which served as a boys' school before the invasion of scientists still stands. Barracks and rows of suburban-style houses line the streets which have names like Pajarito and Oppenheimer. All roads lead out to one-way Civil Defense areas and all areas, on either side, are marked EXPLO-SIVES NO TRESPASSING.

It is difficult to imagine the tar paper shacks of forty years ago, the excitement that gripped everyone who lived in the Secret City. At night physicists and chemists and engineers from many different countries played Viennese waltzes, danced, and made so many babies that, finally, the Army tried to put restraints on reproduction. Oppenheimer watched sunsets; Fermi led his colleagues out on picnics. Mostly, they worked like madmen to make Little Boy which fell eventually on Hiroshima.

I wandered around, lonely in my lack of orientation to the technology which created the town and defined our era. In the drugstore teen-agers chewed gum and played the juke box. A boy in a bluejean jacket wore a silver ring in his ear.

•   •   •

In spite of my grumbling about isolation, I began to succumb to the seduction of the land. I came to depend on the repetition of tastes and sights and smells, to associate the scent of burning piñon with the feel of the adobe wall beside my bed—strong, rough material warm in the cold and cool in the heat. The glints of golden straw in the adobe mixed in my mind with the taste of hot chili peppers; and the burning in my throat with the look of lined faces that have gazed, for centuries, at the mesas.

I visited the chapel during the winter, and, driving there, I felt an exhilaration from the shadows, the trees, the snow, and the adobe along the way. I came to believe I knew what lay on the other side of the mountain. The landscape catapulted my mind into many different places; questions and puzzles darted at me in clear configurations. The chapel had a message—or so I thought—that included me, and I wanted to be included. I was never comfortable with either of the Westphalls, but I was drawn to the chapel. It was a connection to the world, to the war, and even in all its isolation, it was a hieroglyphic of the times.

So, when Dr. Westphall called me and said that they were having a ceremony there to commemorate the truce in Vietnam, I was pleased to go. I took my son Joshua with me.

The service took place at 11:00 on February 3, 1973. The peace treaty had been violated consistently since it was signed, but people came anyway, to celebrate an end to something. A choir from Albuquerque came in a bus. Dr. Westphall, wearing a blue-and-white ski cap, had cotton stuffed in his ears. He greeted people as they arrived. His wife was not there. He went to some length to explain that she had fixed her hair the night before, but, because of a call from her sister who was ill, she had become upset, and he hadn't insisted that she come. His friend, a colonel from California, towered over him.

Snow lay on Wheeler Peak behind us. The ground we stood on was wet and cold. We listened to the choir and said the Lord's Prayer. Dr. Westphall gave a brief address with one mention of a "futile war." Several ministers spoke, and one of them referred to us as "ants on a hill." There was no sense on the knoll of victory or of defeat, of loss or of gain.

In the midst of the ceremony four military jets raced over us, paying tribute to the truce. The colonel from California, who was in the air force, had helped make arrangements for them to come. In a land where one seldom sees an airplane, they looked like something from a film, or science fiction. They came at us from behind, swooped down with a tremendous roar, circled far away over the mountains. Joshua was terrified, clutched at me, and wanted to go inside, but the chapel was locked, so we took shelter in its curved entranceway until the attack was over. During the second pass one plane shot ahead of the others—a gesture, supposedly, in memory of fallen comrades, but, also, for all the dead. At least that was the way Dr. Westphall explained it later. I thought maybe it was a mistake, maybe one of the pilots had gone mad, and I wondered crazily if he was tempted to bomb the chapel.

Throughout the service I watched a Spanish couple who looked as though they were wrapped in a long-standing sorrow. Although the ground around them was mostly bare, the woman, who was wearing thin black shoes, stood the whole time in a patch of snow.

When it was over a woman with frizzy hair, heavy lipstick and a face withered with sadness, went up to embrace Dr. Westphall. I heard her say, "You just never get used to it, do you?"

My son, who had not stopped gripping my hand since the planes came, asked me if they fought in Vietnam with bows and arrows. After I explained, he said he thought that it wouldn't have been so bad if only two or one had died. I thought that he might always confuse peace with jets, so I asked if he knew what peace meant. He said, "It means the country is filled with cities and the trees are tall." He asked if the planes had bullets. Then he asked me to tell him what was written on the markers and we walked along and I read him every name. Our hands were cold because we had forgotten our mittens.

From that day on I felt confused about the chapel. I kept wondering why the old man's wife had not come and what the chapel, which was supposed to have been her idea, meant to her. After that, I returned to it with a sense of curiosity more than of affection. Each time I drove up its driveway I heard the jets roar overhead; and when I stood in its shadow, I thought of shattered families.

Seven

I heard jet whine in the wind that night when I had decided to sleep there. I waited for the old man to return with his friend. I felt as though I was in a bunker, not a cave.

Memory had made me forgetful and I had let the fire dwindle. I stood up to stoke it just as the old man walked through the door to the unfinished back room. Behind him came a tall young man who looked as though he had stepped out of an ad for his generation—rimless glasses, tight-fitting jeans, maroon-and-blue striped velour shirt, and work boots. His dark blond hair was damp, perhaps from a shower, and it curled forward beneath one ear lobe. His mustache was a shade darker than his hair. His eyes were deep blue and looked older than his face.

"This is Matt Hill," said the old man. "He's working with

me at the ranch." He hovered, like a mother introducing
children.

I wondered how I looked, so I put out my hand. I do that
when I can't think what else to do, when I need an extra
instant to size the person up. It surprises men—they don't
expect women to shake hands. But I didn't look at Matt Hill
when he took my hand. I don't know if he smiled, but I know
that he stood there, not moving, like a light.

"Matt was in Vietnam," said the old man.

Of course, I thought, the eyes. "Oh," I responded, au-
tomatically, "when?"

"I got out in '69." He spoke with a slight stammer.

Jesus! By 1969 David Westphall was dead. I didn't know
what to say, so I excused myself and went into the bathroom
and sat on the cold seat of the chemical john. I wondered
what Matt Hill was doing there, why the old man had
brought him up here, what he had told him about me. I
decided not to look in the mirror and then I stood up and
peered into it in the semidarkness, to see how bloodshot my
eyes were. I combed my hair with my fingers, feeling an
edge—a jump in the guts. It had started when Matt Hill
walked into the room, and I didn't like it.

I had loved, for awhile, a man who was a medic and used
heroin in Vietnam, kicked the habit at home, and filled the
void with whatever else he could get his hands on. We spent
a week at the beach once, smoking dope, drinking wine, and
sniffing cocaine. We never ate and rarely slept. One morning we decided to look at the sunrise, went out, and walked
down the road in search of the sun which was rising silently
behind us.

I had lived, for awhile, with an ex-marine who tried to

hang himself from a tree in the backyard. Those men attracted a part of me that I disliked and suspected—the part
that fancies holding hurt and anger in my arms. I had vowed
to look for healthier companions. I bought a house, lived
again in the east, alone with my children. We were wary,
but we were all right, and we read together in my big bed at
night.

Full of resolve, I tucked my tee shirt into my bluejeans so
that my breasts would look attractive, and walked back into
the room. The men were sitting by the fire. They seemed
not to notice me. They were talking about preparing the
ranch for skiers who would come across the pass with Texas
money and space boots to wind down through the old sigh-
ing spruces. In addition to skiing, they would visit the
Pueblo, buy turquoise, go back feeling that they had not
been quite at home in their neighboring state, that something was not quite right, not quite American, about New
Mexico. The old man complained about the people who had
bought the ranch from him, and who were at home in Texas
while he was here, managing things.

I sat down beside the fire, swept the room with my eyes in
order to take another look at Matt Hill. He looked straight at
the old man without glancing in my direction. I figured he
probably wanted to look at me, but then again, I wasn't sure.
He said something about clearing out a ski run between
some pine trees, and I noticed that he spoke with a hint of
the south. I listened to his speech more closely than I did to
his words. I always wonder where stammers come from,
especially in aggressive people. A man who stammers at-
tracts me.

The fire was hot and it made me sleepy. Their talk drifted

beside me. It was hunting season again, deep November, and along the streams that day I had seen men in fluorescent vests, on horseback, guns across their saddles. I thought about the American fall postcard: cars sporting dead deer, their heads lolling over the windows, eyes wide open, deep brown, crimson slits showing along their bellies. There was blood all over the trunks of the Fords and the Chevies and the engines of the Volkswagens. I shunted aside a voice which sneered, you'll stop being so precious about killing animals when you're hungry.

I began to dream of the highway, of lumpy buslike cars with whole families on the move, possessions piled up, like refugees. Recently a family had died in their van on the side of the highway near Albuquerque; the news said they had starved. Everywhere I had been in the past months people talked of hunger, of cutting down, holing in, of plummeting values, and of gardens and canning and sewing. Voices were quiet and scared. How would we get through it? Forgotten grandparents suddenly seemed like sages. I sought out old ladies who could tell me how to make pickles and I read everything I could find about compost and recycling. In the morning I fed my children kasha instead of Captain Crunch.

"Are you asleep?" The old man sounded reproachful.

I straightened up and shook my head, feeling guilty that I hadn't joined in their talk.

"I suppose we should be going . . . let you get some sleep." He got slowly to his feet. Matt Hill didn't move. I wondered what he would do.

The old man gathered up some clothes and put them into a flight bag, pulled the couch seat up, folded it out into a

bed. The mattress was covered with a plastic sheet. Matt
Hill looked at me and asked if I would like to have a glass of
wine. I nodded, and he said that he would go down to the
ranch later. The old man opened his mouth as though he
were going to say something, but that was all. I felt a slit in
my heart watching him bend into the wind.

We stood at the end of the room and gazed into the
blinding lights which beat against the chapel's stucco prow.
The building sat there like a calendar and a prediction of
death—the monument which will be rooted there when the
next round of coffins comes home in planes, gets loaded on
trains, and lowered electronically into fresh-spaded dirt in
the cities and towns across America.

Matt Hill spoke quietly. "In the valley the cowboys call it
a rocketship." He grinned. "When a greenhorn comes, they
tell him there are ICBMs buried underneath it."

"What are they?"

He explained that they were intercontinental ballistic
missiles and he said it in a gentle way, not condescending,
the way people can be when they are telling you something
you really ought to know. I said, "Oh, yeah," as though I
really might have known, and just forgotten. I was a little bit
ashamed for not knowing, and for pretending, so I went to
the table and got the wine.

I told myself that I was a grown-up, and I didn't have to
follow every attraction, like a kid chasing each escaped
balloon. I should have been turning in for a good night's rest.
I hadn't come here to talk to any man, particularly not to a
Vietnam veteran. While I lectured myself, I unrolled the old
man's beat-up, jungle-green sleeping bag and spread it

across the end of the bed. The plastic sheet was out of tune with the wind, out of taste with the wine.

The bed was not as wide as a double. I stood back, expecting him to sit on the bag. He gestured at it, inviting me to sit down. There was not enough space to sit on the floor between the end of the bed and the fire. Finally, "Go ahead," I said.

"No, please."

"There's plenty of room."

Simultaneously we started to sit, stopped, burst out laughing, and both sat down.

"Hey," his eyes narrowed, with laughing, to blue slits, "let's do that again."

"We'd have," I gasped, "to practice for weeks!"

He took off his glasses and wiped his eyes. He looked happy and I wanted to say, let's run outside, hold each other tight, and roll over and over and over all the way down the hill. We each caught our breath. The fire chirruped. My legs warmed; my back felt cold and forlorn.

I asked Matt Hill how he came to be at the ranch, working for the old man. "I decided to drift for awhile," he answered, stammering again. Of course, I thought, there are vets drifting in and out of every crevice of the country. "I had broken up with my girl," he went on. "I was in Texas and I met the owners of the ranch. They said there was work and skiing, so I came on."

We sat in one attitude—arms along our thighs, legs slightly apart, bodies inclined toward the fire. He told me that he came, originally, from Florida, and then from Oklahoma. I asked how long he planned to stay.

"I don't know. I want to ski, but it's a pretty lonely place. Westphall needs help; there's a lot to get done here. He keeps asking me if everything's all right, so I guess he needs me pretty bad. What about you? If you don't mind me saying so, it's a strange place to be staying all alone."

"Oh," I stalled, "it's a long story."

"He was real excited this afternoon, came down and told us a lady writer was coming from New York. I thought you'd be an old lady, or a librarian, or something. I was surprised when I saw you."

I nodded, hid my face which lights up at an indirect compliment, flares at a direct one. "I guess there's not much to do around here."

"Sometimes I go to the bar in Eagle Nest, but it's mostly cowboys, real hokey. The guy I bunk with at the ranch talks till he falls asleep. I wouldn't talk to him anyway."

I reminded myself of the consequences of a late night. I dreaded burning eyes, difficulty talking to the old man, failed purpose. I didn't want to have to stay there another night. It wasn't sensible to stay up any longer. But the wind tore at the knoll which fell away behind us, and Matt Hill's hands were tanned and his fingers were long with large white nails. He held his glass between them, moving it slightly now and then. I guessed that he had been a Marine. He had the manner—gentleness grown out of knowing brutality, a wary way of looking. I wondered where his hands had been.

Attraction is not sensible. It's like being in a heated pool where you slip back, continually, to the place where the hot water pours in. Time changes. You go limp, aware only of that stream at your back. You drift away, and you return.

"Westphall said you were writing something about the chapel."

I looked around the room, as though someone, something might be listening. "Not about the chapel, really."

"Oh, yeah? That's just as well."

"How come?"

"It's spooky."

"That's probably a reason to write about it."

"I don't think so."

"Why not?" I bristled.

"Listen, I slept up here when I first came, before they had a bunk for me at the ranch. I'd rather sleep in the snow than sleep up here again. It's the weirdest goddam place I've ever been."

"Do you think it's sad?" I was suddenly caught up in the story. It dogged me, even in warm pools. I had never heard anyone say a bad word about the chapel before, and I felt, somehow, that I ought to defend it.

"No, it's not sad. There's something wrong in it. Something funny."

"Don't you at least think it's a moving monument to the people who died in Vietnam, and . . ."

"And thank you Barbara Walters . . . this has been the . . ."

I was embarrassed, and I had to laugh. He laughed too, but I could tell he was looking at me to see if he had hurt my feelings. He raised his hand, as if to touch my arm, and dropped it. He spoke coldly, quietly, as though he were trying to explain something frightening to a child.

"Look, this place is the last thing any of those guys would have wanted."

"But why?"

"There's not a guy over there who would have wanted this place to be built in his name. If I had died, I would never have wanted my photograph in there," he inclined his head toward the chapel. "It's all death; there's no life to it."

I sat still. I felt sick. He was either dumb, or crazy, or he was right. I heard the anger in his voice and I had heard it before. I felt as though he had run a bayonet through my story.

I watched him, out of the corner of my eye. How did I know he wasn't a lunatic? I knew the facts: Vietnam vets were murderers, robbers, suicides, woman beaters, dopers, dealers, pushers, pimps. The press wouldn't let us forget it, and I had contributed to it by writing about their troubles. The stories were legion. In Dallas a vet held up a Seven-Eleven, shot the telephone off the wall; in L.A. another one took hostages, then begged them to call the cops before he hurt anyone; in Philly a Medal of Honor winner cleaned out a bank. In the same city a young ex-army man whose most violent act had been to drop a cherry bomb in a toilet in fourth grade, beat up his wife in the middle of the night, and no one thought to do anything about it. No one said to him, yes, this is happening all over and there are people you can talk to, to help it not happen again. So whatever was wrong stayed buried, turned malignant, grew so big it popped through his skin. Another night, he broke into the apartment of a young woman who refused to dance with him in a bar. She fought against him and ended in a hospital, broken, bruised, missing an eye. He will be in prison for a long, long time.

Matt Hill turned to me and said, gently, "I'm keeping you up. You must be tired."

"Oh, a little," I said lightly. "But we could have one more glass of wine."

He filled our glasses. If I could have spoken the truth to him, I would have said, knowledge breeds fear and you scare me. After I studied the crime rate in New York City, I was more afraid to walk home at night than I had been before. When two quaking teen-age junkies held me up with a filed butcher knife in my elevator, I thought, how inevitable. I saw them as a statistic and I behaved well. Then I went to bed and had convulsions. After that I never rode the elevator alone, tried never to walk ahead of anyone on the street, even in the daytime. And, partly, I will always be afraid because I know that some men beat women up when they come home from a war where women died like flies. I know that men who have appeared normal for years can suddenly become violent. Knowing these things is not frightening in the same way as sitting beside the hands that once were fists. And thinking of them spread across my breasts.

I am easy to talk to, easy to make love to. They are connected. Usually it doesn't matter which comes first, but love without talk is as empty as the valley below, where cars seldom stop at the log cabins by the lake, where no boats float, where waves wash over no one.

We watched the fire in silence. After awhile I got up and lit the candle shaped like a Mayan bowl. The wind hammered at the sides of the bunker. I felt my eyes somewhere near the back of my skull, and I knew that they were burnt crimson with exhaustion. Suddenly it grew dark beyond the door. The chapel lights had gone out. I caught my breath, "Look!" Matt Hill chuckled. "It's O.K. They turn off at 10:00. In the valley they say it's magic." I wondered how the old man could sleep up here, night after night. Or did he love the tumbleweed hurtling across the hill, the camomile twisting, the moon colder than snow? I went back and sat down beside him, hungry for human warmth, and I wrapped myself in my arms.

Matt Hill turned and turned his glass, watching it in his hands between his knees. I sat in the identical position, only I held my glass still. I tried to imagine how he would begin to make love. Every man is different—some brusque, some light, some awkward. I have never known a man who wasn't shy. New Women don't like to admit it, but they understand that shyness and capitalize on it. They want to say that an advance is a powerplay; they know it is the end-product of frustration. I thought that Matt would be slow and very gentle. He would have to take off his glasses. He did nothing to mask his shyness so he attracted me at all levels: woman—mother—girl. I arched back to reality, which was that he had not touched even my little finger, and asked him what he had done since he came home from the war.

He looked at me, smiled bitterly. "When I first got home no one paid much attention to me. They were just going on with their lives. Guys in my fraternity sort of shied away from me. My girl friend left me. I went to this psychiatrist for a while, but it didn't help much. I went to Park Ranger training. When I got out, there was a job available and I was qualified, but they gave it to a draft–resister who had just come back from Canada. Made me feel real bad, you know? I had a lot of problems, I guess. I couldn't get it straight about all those guys dying over there and me being alive. I guess it sounds silly."

"No, it doesn't."

I had heard it in a hundred interviews. Men who shared experiences in Vietnam came home, not knowing that their experiences at home would be common to many of them. Shot back into their small-town slots, their unemployment lines, their schools, their changed relationships, their dim rooms lit by the silver of nationwide TV, a psychic web binds them. A haunted memory makes them nod and say, sure, that figures, when a vet blows someone away, or steals a car, or holds up a bank, or drives ninety miles an hour into a tree. Matt's guilt resides in thousands of souls, but mostly it sits there, silently. They think they are strange.

"It doesn't sound silly," I said again. "Lots of guys feel that way." My hands felt limp, my voice weak. What was I going to do, deliver a lecture on Post-Vietnam-Syndrome, cite Robert Jay Lifton, suggest a rap group here in the hills of New Mexico, type out a reading list? Does it make a man feel better to know that other people feel just as shitty as he does? "Look," I said, "everyone I've talked to feels that way. It's even got a name—it's called survivor guilt."

He looked at me warily. He took off his glasses, rubbed the lenses along his thighs. His eyes looked larger and farther away. "I'm a quiet sort of person, hardly ever lost my temper. But after I got back, started living with this girl I . . . well . . . I'd wake up and I'd be beating on her, I mean really beating her like I wanted to kill her. . . ." His voice was pinched with pain. I wanted to run. I saw myself opening the door facing the valley and rushing out to gulp the textured air. I wanted to get away. I had heard it before. I hear until I am afraid that I will listen and not hear anymore. I have only myself to blame: I've made it my business. I open my ear and for every open ear there is a scream waiting to force its way in.

"Sometimes," he went on, "I'd get up and beat on the wall, but other times I had already hurt her before I knew what I was doing."

He had begun to trust me, I could tell. Now he would talk all night.

"I'd get so angry in my dreams, just angry like hot flashes of anger. I'm not even sure what the dreams were about. . . ."

I do not know what it is like to be alone with a memory of violence, but I think it must be one of the loneliest feelings in the world. I said simply that the same kind of thing had happened to other men, and that the worst course is to avoid talking about it.

"I've never talked about it before. . . . You're easy to talk to."

An empty victory. My face is sweet and my hands are open. My power, however, lies in your talk; I stalk you with my listening. I have a large space for your stories and I can listen, immobile, reptilian, for hours. But, Matt, listen, while you talk, my attention slides away. Part of me doesn't want to hear or care. It crawls away and lies blocking the border of the empty space, greenish, nasty, greedy, gray. With the tiniest effort, I get you to talk, to trust me, and only part of me is there.

The other part paces up and down this strange room in this bunker, nestled like a bomb in the chapel's shadow. Paces and rants, hunting down the story, seeing you as a barrier between it and myself and, at the same time, beginning to believe I cannot tell it without you. I want you to go away; I imagine my hand on your arm, and I remember that in a day I will be gone and you will be back at the ranch, working under the driven eye of the old man, and that there is something dead-end about a few hours of love-making. Still I want you to stay.

He bent toward the fire and his arm leaned into mine. Leaning is full of longing; it moves me in a nameless way. A boy leans against a man's arm in a bus, an old woman leans down on her cane, a young woman leans into a man's chest, a dead tree leans against a living one. My fantasy of a lap recurs, a mothering lap where I can throw myself down, lean into the warmth, and feel despair drift away. I have never found it; if I did, the fantasy would die. Instead I am tall and built to be leant against, so Matt's arm didn't surprise me; it warmed my skin, not my heart.

I followed his need to talk the way I follow my children in the park. He darted—here to home to Danang to here— settled in Florida. "I really liked her. I still do, I'm getting over it, I guess. I only knew her about six months but it was pretty heavy. It was just . . . I guess it sounds silly . . . well, she kept on making remarks about the Corps, like anyone who went in the Marines must be crazy, or mean. Like every guy over there had murdered babies and raped women. I tried to explain. Sometimes I'd think she under- stood, then another remark would pop out. I talked to my buddy about it, and he talked to her. It didn't do much good. Finally, I left. She called before I came up here, I just said I was going away. . . ."

Stories of loss—you can only gaze into space with horri- fied eyes and swallow your trite responses. Matt's story was straightforward, yet its implications swam in front of me, twisted and complex. Pain came through his pores and there was nothing to catch it with. I wasn't going to do it. People are paid to do that nowadays. It *used* to be what women were for. I get paid to listen, goddamit, don't tell me any more. I don't want to feel sorry. I don't want to sit here wanting to take you in my arms. I want you to go away.

I kept not wanting to hear as I asked to hear more. Like the woman who screams NO! pulling the man down on top of her. My mother used to lie in the bathtub and cry and tell me how mean my father was to her. I sat on the bath mat beside the tub and listened, full of eight-year-old fear. If I had said, don't, I don't want to hear, I love him, I would have been saved. Maybe. But, I heard it all and I learned to

package the pain—open one at a time: Sunday was the
he's–never–at–home box, Monday was the he's–always–
picking–on–me one. I let it ferment. Then it comes on, full
force, like the return of a ragged dream. I have learned to
hear as much as I can bear. I write down the rest, or store it.
I am addicted.

I reached out and took Matt's glass, walked to the table,
and refilled it. I returned and sat down. It would be better to
touch one another. I knew he thought so too, but something
sat between us and shared our wine.

Matt smiled at me. His eyes were alive again, as though
talking had dampened and then rekindled them. "I've
talked a lot about myself. I don't know anything about you."

"Me?" Listening is my forte. I avoid talking, particularly
about myself. What could I say? I'm a journalist of sorts, a
collector of tales, I suppose, an ear which unwinds what it
holds like a tape unwinds its truth and its lies, puts them into
paragraphs for people to read and forget. I am part of that
unconnected and self-suspecting band of hunters which
combs the continent for information to enlighten our desperate days and describe our destiny. We cross and recross
the country, looking for answers, examining our compa-
triots, hoping that bizarre events and out-of-the-way people
will tell us why we're so fucked up when we started out so
fine.

I panic when someone says, "Well now, let's talk about
you." I'm a master at shifting the talk back to the questioner.
I went to a psychiatrist once, used to think for days about
what I wanted to say, tried to say it in an amusing fashion
until for the third session in a row he fell asleep and I never

went back and never paid the bill. He saw my name in a magazine, tracked me down, but I never answered him. I wonder if he's still nodding off in his old, high-backed Naugahyde chair.

But tricks and avoidances seemed shoddy that evening so I tried to answer as honestly as I could. I said, "I grew up in a cellophane bag."

"How do you mean?"

I told him about the Midwest, the Lake, about believing in the tall, the strong, and the good. "During the war I was in the peace movement, I did draft counselling, marched, licked envelopes. I used to feel glad when an American plane was shot down, and guilty about feeling glad. I had no idea what war was like. I didn't know anyone who went; I thought GIs were the enemy. Later, I went to an army hospital and interviewed amputees. I got to know some of them and we became friends. One of them, who is still my friend, told me that he had wanted to go to Canada instead of Vietnam, but his Dad had said if he didn't go, he could never come home again. So he went, and he lost both his legs. His Dad came to see him in the hospital and said, 'You've proved you're a man.' I guess you could say I'm a peacenik turned complicated."

Matt Hill told me that when he was a boy, he went to see movies about the Second World War and that he used to stand up in the theater and cover his heart when they played the national anthem. He used to cry, secretly, when he thought about the men who had saved our country. "I thought I would gladly die for this," he said.

I said, "Part of me still feels that way, can you believe it?

After all we've learned, after all that's happened, can you believe it?"

Matt Hill nodded. He took off his glasses again, wiped his eyes, although I hadn't seen a tear. I knew what caused it, if it was a tear, because I had a lump in my throat, and the room had an odor of loss.

We sat, without moving, watching the dying fire, legs lined up, denim touching denim, lightly.

Eight

Something was wrong. We were trapped there, somewhere between the valley and the tops of the mountains. We were caught there in our jeans and our twentieth-century boots. We were tall and slim and our stomachs were full of wine. But we were paralyzed, somehow, dead as David whose picture hung midpoint in the line-up on the chapel wall.

I asked Matt Hill about working at the ranch.

"I have a hard time working for anyone, but Westphall's O.K. to work for—so far. He works harder than everyone else put together."

I shuddered.

"Sometimes it's weird, like the other day there's three guys my age helping him. We're supposed to dig out this big tank full of shit, get down in it and all. Well, no one wants to, so he jumps in and starts shovelling. No one can pay me to do that. Then he calls to us to haul him out, and after we do, he starts telling us that if we just hold him by the legs, he can extend his body straight out and hold it there." He held out his hand, even as a plane. "He puts a lot of stock in the place, that's for sure. He works his tail off at the ranch, then he comes up to the chapel and keeps on till he drops."

I remembered a letter the old man had written, describing his work on the chapel in a furious wind, in freezing weather. He had been plastering the peak of the chapel, standing on a sixty-foot-high scaffold on top of which he had placed a stool David had made when he was in the Boy Scouts. The letter had concluded:

> On the stool is the sixty-year-old, 140-pound father of the deceased veteran. The furious wind has just blown off his stocking cap and his bald head is exposed to the freezing elements. He is plastering the highest point of the Chapel. On the ground are three men each young enough to be the old man's son. They do not join him because they are afraid. The old man understands because he is also afraid, but his son's handiwork beneath his feet has given him strength and courage.

I had felt sad and somehow disgusted as I read that letter. "He has to work hard," I said now. "He's competing with a dead man."

Matt Hill stared at me. After a moment, he said, "That sounds kind of weird."

I wanted to sleep, but his eyes were full of flares from the firelight, and his hair looked like it was tinted with left-over

sun. I could, I thought, place my index finger on the inside
of his wrist, run it lightly down the length of his thumb.
Instead, I asked him if it was difficult for him to work for
people because of the lifers in Vietnam.

"Why did you ask?" His eyes narrowed on me.

I shrugged. "I've talked to a lot of vets."

"I didn't even realize it till I got to Nam. I hated the lifers
before, but it wasn't like I wanted to kill every one I saw.
That didn't begin till the time there was a fragging—at least
an attempt at one. A guy threw a grenade at a lifer." He
spoke quickly, lips close together, without the stammer.
"The guy screwed up, killed an enlisted man instead of the
lifer. We were in the field. They made us stand in the
perimeter—stand there for *three hours,* with our arms in
the air. While I was standing there, sweating like a pig, it
came over me, like, here I am, fighting this filthy war for
these motherfuckers. After that, everything was different."

Matt Hill kicked the fire to stir it up and threw a log on top
of the embers. Smoke curled toward us.

"I guess I still don't know what you're doing here," he
changed the subject, avoiding me.

How could I explain? I hardly knew myself, except that I
had been following an instinct, watching the chapel and the
man who built it. I had been a spy on the mountainside. I
had gone after the old man's guts with a pickax and I had
tried to befriend his son, a dead man. I had tried to track
them back to their mothers' wombs, and I had come away
with despair at the silence of the dead and anger at the
complexity of the living.

"I'm a friend of the Westphalls," I said, lamely.

"You know her then?"

I nodded. I thought of her, alone on the horizon that stretched multitudes of miles behind the trailer, away from New Mexico out toward the Great Plains, toward the green trees, and lakes, and garden snakes of the Midwest.

"What's she like?"

"Smart."

"I got the idea she was kind of strange."

"It's a long story."

"She never comes here."

"She probably never will again."

"Why not?"

Suddenly, as if at a signal, the wind stopped blowing. Try to imagine: a full orchestra, in the midst of a symphony, stops; the sea, crashing against a cliff, ceases. I strained to hear it. I had steeled myself against it, the way you do against cold, and, in that manner, I had got onto a keel with it. Now I felt nervous, and deprived. Matt said, "That happens up here. Don't worry."

"I'm not. It's just that I feel like the wind went out of the sail," I laughed nervously. "It's thrown me off."

"When I slept up here I woke up everytime it happened. I tell you, I'd never sleep here again."

I shivered. A long shiver down to my soles.

He pressed me, "What's the deal? Why won't she come back to the chapel?"

Fatigue, like a drug, had fallen on me. "I don't know if I can tell you. It's complicated."

"The other day the old man called me David."

I got up and walked past the boarded-up windows, down

to the door, and peered out at the dark form of the chapel. His voice trailed me, "I'd like to know about him."

"It'll take forever." I spoke at the door, almost shouting.

He didn't answer. I looked back at him, had a swift vision of him squatting in a trench somewhere I couldn't imagine, waiting for forever.

I sat down in the old man's armchair.

"When David Westphall was a little boy, his favorite book was *Wings for Per*, a story about a boy who grows up and becomes a pilot in the war. His mother gave it to him while his father was in the Pacific. When he went to Vietnam, the family was living here at the ranch. Just before he left, he gave most of his books to the local school library, but he gave the old copy of *Wings for Per* to his mother and said, 'I can't give away this book. It's worth a million other books.'

"Now, listen, the end of that book says, 'Then I will fly up into the clear, washed air of spring and soar over the eagle's nest and over my home under the crag. Mother will stand in front of the house and clasp her hands in wonder. She will say, "Look, Per has wings." ' "

"Jesus!"

I went on, relentlessly. "In high school he loved a book about a Greek warrior. He read about Washington and Lincoln. He read voraciously. He grew up in the forties and fifties, in the eye of the Red-hating storm. He got older and read Ayn Rand. In the Marine Corps he read Eric Hoffer. He was a patriot. Once we were all patriots. He called himself a Unitarian. Whatever he was, he was a believer. He wrote to his brother that God had made him from the Marine Corps officer mold."

Suddenly I felt angry at David and angrier at Matt Hill. "What is it anyway," I asked sourly, "about being a Marine?"

Matt Hill walked toward me. He looked at me as though he felt superior to me, pitied me, and felt ashamed of himself all at the same time. "A Marine," he said, "is unimpeachable."

That was it, then.

I searched my life for a parallel, and the only thing I could find was the kind of sacredness of being pregnant and of having a new baby. But the parallels were so diametrically opposed that I felt I was looking with eyes too crooked to see in the same direction. I leaned back in the armchair and was silent.

The wind cried at the walls.

Matt Hill stood at the door, looking out at the blackness. "Why," he asked, without turning around, "did he join the Marine Corps?"

I writhed under the burden of facts, the insecurity of my lack of solid answers. I began again, lifelessly, as though I were reciting a laundry list.

"I suppose that David's brother knows more about him than anyone else."

Doug Westphall had come to see me in Taos in the spring of the year I lived there. He had just gotten out of the air force. He sat very straight in a chair in my room, hands folded in his lap. He looked like a beautiful, trapped rabbit and he answered my questions with difficulty.

He talked, like his father, in a monotonous, measured manner:

"Dad made a lot of money in the fifties. He built a ridiculously fabulous house in the mountains outside Albuquerque, a place called Juan Tabo. He was deathly ill at the time. He doesn't like cities and he has idiosyncracies—dogs barking bother him, the sound of cars drives him crazy. Certain radio announcers bother him so much we have to turn the radio off. In the fifties he wasn't so much tired, the way he is now, but he had standards and he was intolerant towards people not able to live up to them. . . ."

Matt Hill interrupted. "I guess there's not a man in his twenties or thirties in this country who couldn't say the same thing about his father."

"What about women?"

"I thought they all loved their papas right to death," he mock-drawled, grinning.

I pretended to ignore him, remembering the way Doug's dark eyes blinked and grew moist, like his father's, from time to time. I had asked him about his and David's childhood:

"We were always building something," he had replied. "As early as 1952 we worked on Dad's projects during summers and after school. My father was big on having us build brush-and-rock dams across the arroyos to prevent erosion from flash-flooding. This activity lasted many years and resulted in dozens of dams, anywhere from one foot high by five feet long, up to one which was about three feet high and thirty wide. David really didn't care for this activity.

"We were isolated at Juan Tabo. We had, of course, to commute to school. We were in the habit of waving to all truckers and keeping a tabulation—over many months that amounted to hundreds of waves—of what percentage waved back. Sounds strange, but we used to get quite excited about it.

"We used to send money to CARE for their overseas packages. David used to feel that such activities represented true religion.

"We got paid for working on Dad's projects, and we put our savings into an expensive and ornate series of toy soldiers. Redcoats and Indians and Civil War troops. We bought them in Albuquerque at a toy and yarn shop. We had big battles, built forts and lined them up and had maneuvers and tactics on the hillside by our house. We had a battle area of ten square yards.

"I don't recall who won.

"We let them lie there and rot.

"In the fifties we were always in combat games—swords, garbage can lids, guns, cowboys and Indians. We had two horses, rode them bareback and with a saddle blanket.

"I remember one time David fell off one of the horses, a gelding named Cimarron, while riding downhill bareback. The horse was running fast and David's head hit a rock when he fell. Dad was quite upset and concerned and angry. He took David to Albuquerque. As I recall, the cut required stitches.

"I know it sounds strange, but we didn't eat at the table with our parents. David and I ate at the breakfast bar. Chewing noises bothered Dad a lot. He singled out David to reprimand for these things; even in his voice he would criticize him.

"In fact, Dad arranged for us to have singing lessons

because David's voice bothered him so much. He thought that David should learn to control it. It never seemed to me that there was anything wrong with David's voice.

"Mother was always in the background, as a kind of mediator. Sometimes Dad would treat her like an equal, sometimes he would act as though she was inferior. We were always aware that he had degrees, and she had gone only to twelfth grade.

"David and I had a visual understanding about the pressures. Like if Dad would urge David to do something he didn't want to do, and he wouldn't rebel, we knew empathetically what the other felt. This lasted all his life.

"Even when we were very young, Dad would get involved in adult football games and take us along. David could participate more than I. There was never a lot of talking and understanding other than those connected with athletics.

"As an athlete David was considered super—big and fast and strong."

Matt Hill snorted. "I'll bet the old man loved that!"

"Maybe he was jealous."

"Fucking A." He had started to pace around between the bed and the fire. He looked different from the way he had awhile ago—there was a sharper set to his jaw and his neck craned toward the floor.

"Well," I asked. "Which? Proud or jealous?"

"Both. Don't you see?"

I had seen it with mothers and daughters: the mother teaches her secrets and then, one day, sees all the beauty transferred into the younger face. It's investing and being robbed at the same time. It occurred to me that the old man was terrified of being old.

I was picking the burrs off me and sticking them on Matt Hill and I was almost sorry. But he was not my victim; he was an accomplice. Together we were finding the story of the boy who ate at the breakfast bar.

The old man had had to pit himself against his own father, had nearly killed himself just to get to play ball in high school, and suddenly, he had a star son, growing taller than himself, getting top grades, making touchdowns, growing up gentle, and kind, and good-looking. He must have feared him as much as he prized him. Like all stars, he was the hope and he was the hate.

I explained to Matt Hill that the old man, his wife and Doug had all told their versions of the story of David's football career.

> JEANNE: In football Victor wanted David to be the best. He intruded on the coach's business. He showed him pictures and compared David to the other boys.

> VICTOR: I helped, talked, coached. When David was in high school, I watched the practices. Possibly that interest affected the coach's attitude. They made him a tackle even though he was the fastest runner. The director of the athletic system questioned the coach and they changed him to backfield the evening before the first game. Then he made a touchdown. Maybe I had too much interest. Maybe my interest and resentment over the way he was treated made trouble for him.

"Maybe!" Matt Hill sneered. He looked as though he disliked me. I knew what he disliked was the story, but it made me nervous.

DOUG: The football prejudice against David started when he was a junior. He was naturally a back but they made him a tackle. Dad was infuriated, but I don't think he spoke to the coach. The coach used to come to our house to work out with weights and Dad used to show off feats with the weights which the coach couldn't do.

Of course, it's conceivable that they thought David was clumsy, but after awhile they put him in backfield.

In junior high and high school Dad would always come to our practices and he got to be friendly with the coaches. The tragedy was that he didn't want David to excel in sports so much for David as for himself. He got vicarious rewards through David. He got those things he didn't have a chance to achieve while he was young. Hence the strong pressures.

Dad has had to fight for everything he has. He's still insecure, even with his doctorate. It was a monumental event in his life, getting that degree, and I suppose that's why he calls himself Doctor, so people will react to it.

David reacted to all this in a reserved sort of way. He was naturally reserved. He was competitive in a calm sort of way. He was good-looking, but he never thought he was attractive enough. I'm sure he was a happy baby, but I don't remember him laughing much, even though he had a good sense of humor. He was always conscious of the relationship between him and my father. Even so, he did enjoy things. He took piano lessons and he was a good player. Sometimes he would practice hours on end. He taught himself to play guitar, flamenco mostly. I remember he had a record by the Ink Spots. He was enthralled by Strauss waltzes—he thought there was nothing comparable to those. We listened to them at Juan Tabo.

David was the only person I was close to. Even so we were never really close. It could have been a close relationship, but it didn't happen. Let's face it, nobody in the family ever expressed much of anything. We were like robots. Now whenever I picture David in situations, like on the battlefield, he's always alone.

Matt Hill's pacing was getting on my nerves so I stood up and walked toward him. He winked at me, gave me a small dry smile. "Pretty much your standard story."

"You wanted to hear it."

"Go on."

"You're making me nervous."

"Sorry." He sat down; his arms hung down between his legs and his face looked wooden.

"David's voice must have become a problem for him. He wrote a letter of self-assessment when he was considering a teaching career: 'Physically, I must improve my voice if I'm to be a successful teacher. Everyone knows from experience that it's hard to take a speaker seriously if he squeaks, drawls, or shows any other kind of vocal inadequacy.' "

At the moment of speaking I realized I was talking to a man with a stammer. His expression didn't change, however, and I went on, mortified. "He wrote that letter in 1964, after he had done his first four years in the Marine Corps. The reasons for his leaving college and going into the

Corps are different, depending on who gives them. David wrote, in the same letter, that he had wanted to go to West Point, had even spent a year in a military academy preparing for entrance there. He did poorly in mathematics and was not accepted. He chose the University of New Mexico in spite of offers of football scholarships from other colleges and, as he put it, 'the appeal of going to a school away from home.' He decided to major in history and then go into high school teaching. 'Although I did well enough in freshman football to start every game, and well enough scholastically to make the dean's list, I was restless, uneasy, and dissatisfied. The next year I quit school and enlisted. . . .'

"He spent four years in Hawaii and Virginia and California, first as an infantryman, then as an MP. Doug said, 'Dad was concerned about David playing service football.' After two years in the Marines he married a girl he had known in high school. He described her as being 'sweet, pretty, and (obviously) intelligent to boot.' His mother said, 'She was a little cutie-pie, roly-poly, from Tennessee. Very attention getting. They were married in Albuquerque and the reception was at the Sandia Base officers club because her father was in the air force. I felt sad.'

"David had written home about his life in the Marine Corps: 'One day in the barracks I was reading *Arrowsmith* and wanted to discuss it with someone. On that entire floor if the majority thought Sinclair Lewis was anyone, they thought he was a barber over in the PX. The only people in that platoon with whom I could talk about the book or its author were two Negroes. This example is typical. On a per capita basis not only were Negro Marines better informed than were whites about jazz and sports, but also about politics, geography, world happenings, and literature. Whites *must* have held an edge in a discussion of automobile engines. (Both races claimed to know all there was to know about women.)' "

I peeked at Matt Hill. He grinned sheepishly. I couldn't look him in the eye, so I got up and looked out the door. Snowflakes angled toward me and I turned off the standing lamp and watched them come, razor sharp. I said, "It's snowing."

I walked to the bed, flopped down, put my arms under my head. I had been talking with a tight jaw.

He was sitting close to me. "I don't want to sound like an old lady," he said gently, "but I don't like you sleeping up here."

"I'll be all right," I said firmly. I was terrified.

He looked at me and something moved inside me. While I was talking, I had plucked and pulled at my hair which was rumpled now around my face and neck.

New Women are supposed to out with it; I want to fuck you, we're supposed to say. Or, more circumspectly: I feel very attracted to you, you know. Or: if you want to make love, it's O.K. with me. Well, I have never said that to anyone in my life. It doesn't mean I won't, or that I haven't wanted to. It scares me. I'm used to being hunted; I'm scared of scaring someone. I'm afraid, too, that someone might say, no, thank you, and that would make me feel ugly, weird, too fat, or too thin, depending on the day. I feel sorry for men, having to do all the pushing. So I try to be gentle. But, then, too, sometimes I go through the motions—

vacuous, fucked, and untouched—and that's not doing any-
one any favors. It's disgusting, in fact—an unliberated lump.
There is a place in between. But none of this helped me with
Matt Hill.

He was still looking at me. I wanted to scream, why don't
you take my hand, or say, "I like your crooked teeth," or
anything at all? What, I wondered, did he want? Was he
sitting here, hour upon hour, to look at me or to hear the
story? Was the story simply a sexual exercise? I saw the
softness in his eyes and I knew he had killed people. That is a
powerful combination.

And how would it be? Images floated like bright fish,
disappeared into fear, reappeared:

He stretches out on his side, props himself on an elbow,
lies facing me. He brushes back his hair on one side—a
nervous gesture. I smile, lie on my side, head down on my
arm outstretched beneath it. He takes off his glasses, puts
them on the floor.

My heart caught, imagining:

It is time to decide and, yet, I don't know whether I will
like his lips; I don't know how his hand will be, on my skin.
And if it is dull, will I be too cowardly to sit up briskly? I lie,
smiling, and waiting, and he spreads his hand along the side
of my face, slides it back toward my ear, making me different
than I was an instant ago. The motion takes away my words,
my past and future, molds me exactly to the moment. There
is room for no one else, for no idea, no deceit. His hand
repeats its movement as mine begins an imitation. He leans
toward me, finds my mouth.

A new mouth is as alien as a foreign land; no matter how

you've studied it, listened to it, you do not know how it's going to feel. Kissing is its own realm; some people kiss better than they make love. Some make love to suit you, but you can do without kissing them. Some people avoid it—something must have been kept from them when they were children.

I see Matt Hill kissing me lightly, pulling back, and looking at me, his eyes smaller and more tired without his glasses, lines on his nose where they had sat. But it must be all right, because his lips come back, and the moment narrows once more into only that: four lines of skin, as different from the face as the underside from the top of a leaf, four lines pushing, narrowing and widening, flattening to nothing but teeth. My breath comes according to his. He moves on top of me and I am scared and I pull my lips away and push my face against his head. His body fits me. His boots hang over the end of the bed, on either side of mine. My feet sweat cold beside the fire. I smooth his head; his hair is soft and smells like smoke of piñon. My heart races in my throat and its echo, far below, competes.

Instead, I looked away, threw my arm across my eyes. I told myself to stop imagining. A log cracked in the fire.

I got up and walked around the room as if I knew why I was doing it. I picked up the Mayan bowl candle and blew it out, sat holding it in the armchair. "Everything here is connected to the chapel."

"That sounds kind of exaggerated. What about you and me? We're just here because we're here. I'm drifting, you're messing around with a story. We could be anywhere."

It hadn't occurred to me that I might not like him at all.

He remained sitting on the bed. "Everything *is* connected to Westphall, I guess."

"It's the same thing," I said tersely. "People built monuments to themselves in the names of other peoples' causes." I felt well defended; I sounded so literary.

Matt Hill stretched out and propped his head on his hand. He studied my face as though it were a map. "You know, I feel like I can be honest. That sounds like bullshit."

I wanted to go, sit beside him, and shove him off the bed. Instead, my arm drew back, paused, shot the candle at the wall behind the fire. Matt's arm intercepted it—a catch as effortless as a lanky kid's over a base.

He put it on the floor, the way I had imagined him setting down his glasses. I felt caught, stifled, between him and the story. Lonely. I felt I was losing my bearings, losing touch with my flesh. He was watching me.

I went back to the glass door, touched the pane, imagining I could feel the pin pricks of snow, realigning myself with the story.

"The point is," he said, "why did David re-up?"

"I don't know, but I'll tell you all I do know. David got out of the Marines and went back to school. At first he studied forestry, but then he went into history. Doug thinks the old man was happy to see him change to history. He didn't try to orient either son toward a profession, even though once he said he'd like to have three doctors in the family.

"After David was discharged, he went to the University of Montana at Missoula with his wife.

Dear Mom and Dad,   June 1, 1964

It's Monday evening and Lynn is up at school trying to get all her painting done before the quarter's over next week. I have all kinds of studying to do for the finals coming up then, but I thought I'd take a minute and write. The weather warms up occasionally, but there's still snow on some of the hills. Yesterday I went out climbing, and looking for flowers to practice identifying for my botany final. Then I came home and exercised a little more. I got up to 84 (consecutive) push-ups. Some days I can barely do 70, but I never have any trouble with 50 like I used to. I've been doing isometric exercises which seems to help. I've found a good place for them: the bathtub. It lends itself to all kinds of exercises. Still, I should do more running than I have been lately."

Right up until he was killed in their deadly competition, David never ceased trying to please his father. Even his letters from Vietnam underline, in a modest way, how responsible he was, how good he was at his job.

Matt Hill walked around, twisting the candle in his hand. "Look, when you join the Corps, only the Corps can criticize you. It's like getting out on a limb that's so high no one even tries to pull you down. It's no one or the big one, no half measures, no way stations, no rest stops. We are the ones who never leave behind our dead."

I noticed that he said "we," and I marvelled at the power of that society of men. For as long as I can recall, it's been planted in my mind that a Marine is special, sort of a god, someone not to mess with. Vietnam made me think it through, but I'm a woman and I wasn't in the war. I could afford to think it through.

"Then David became a Marine to be untouchable?" I asked.

"Mostly that's what we did. Untouchable or dead. It's a way to be."

DOUG: While I was in the air force David got divorced. It shocked me because I never was aware of any conflict or hassles. She seemed like a gentle and decent and easy-going girl and she seemed to really want to get married originally. Once when I went to see them he said a divorce might be in the offing, but he wouldn't say why.

The divorce affected him very deeply. He was crying when my parents brought him back from Missoula. I don't know why Vietnam appealed to him, but I see that he was propelled into the situation. We have to face the possibility that maybe he didn't want to live.

At one time I was considering marriage and he wrote to me from Vietnam: "Dear Doug, . . . I won't be there in November whether you'll be needing my services as a best man or not. But marriage? No, no! You're your own best judge of this, but beware, beware! In any case there are thousands and thousands of women, plus 'world enough and time' . . . don't be hasty. Take care, lad".

After the divorce David was living at home and he went to a psychiatrist in Albuquerque. I think that he wrote me that he had to get away from Dad's influence.

JEANNE: David worked at the Albuquerque Indian hospital in the incoming accident section. I don't know if he was sicker than he thought he was, or what, but he was going to see a psychiatrist.

One afternoon I was on my way home and Victor met me on the road, ordered me to go up to the house and be back down off the mountain in ten minutes. He was mad because he found David sleeping. He had woken him up. Nobody's supposed to sleep in the daytime, according to Victor. So we left, went downtown, and had supper. When we came back, David had packed up and left.

Matt Hill spoke without inflection, "He had to leave, or else he would have killed the old man."

Flakes pelted the door. The fire snapped. I felt shrunken. I had lost my sense of time and I had no watch. The snow said that it was no longer autumn, that it was already winter; even so, I had lost the sense of seasons.

JEANNE: He drove all night all the way to Missoula. Victor was mad because I had bought David a new car instead of a used one. I'd worked and I wanted to give it to him. A Chevrolet convertible Corvair for only $2000. Victor still screams about that.

David never wrote to Victor. He wrote to me at my sister's. Once Victor sent him $500. David lived alone, frugally, washed dishes in a restaurant, loaded lumber into freight cars.

We stayed still in the hissing of the fire. My mind trotted in curlicues. Do men go to war to rout, as well as to pacify, their fathers?

Is a bloody football field, or a bunker, the only refuge from the breath of the old man?

I wish some man would tell me.

When I ask, they shuffle their shoes, change the subject, or say, "I don't know, I haven't thought about it," or just, "Well, maybe."

I said to Matt Hill, "Once I asked the old man whom he blamed for David's death. He said, 'The only possible blame I can find for his death is my own.' "

"Whom would you blame?" Matt looked at me, evilly.

"I've always sort of blamed the so-called war machine— you know, Johnson, Rusk, McNamara, Bundy—the same rotten old crew. What about you? Whom do you blame?"

"What the fuck am I going to say? The founding fathers? You know, I've had my thoughts. When I first got home, I used to think about walking through homes—apartments, and houses, and condominiums—just walking through, tossing grenades. Mostly I stay away from places where I get the feeling people are to blame."

I got up and took the candle out of his hand.

"If you're going to throw it again, warn me," he laughed, and I pretended not to hear. We sat down, facing each other across the room.

"What was Westphall doing in his war?" he asked.

"Setting up post offices in the Pacific."

"Combat?"

"No, I don't think so."

"Figures."

"Why?"

"Don't you understand? Combat is it, the ticket. The old

man didn't get it. What else was David going to do?"

"He always tells me he wishes he had written David and said he wished he could be with him, fighting right along with him. He says, 'I'm in good enough shape. I could have kept up with the best of them.' "

"Sure."

"But he never urged David to go to Vietnam. Doug says he wouldn't have minded if they'd gone to Canada. He never laid his own military career on them."

"But he's military through and through."

"When David and Doug were kids, they all went to Washington, D.C. They went to see the Marine Corps Memorial, the flag-raising at Iwo Jima."

"Yup, uncommon valor is a common virtue."

"And Doug wrote to me: 'My father's great-grandfather died while a POW at Andersonville. My mother's great-grandfather died in action while serving as a Union soldier. One of my mother's uncles was killed in action during World War I, another suffered throughout his life as a result of the aftereffects of gas poisoning. One of my father's cousins died in action during World War II . . .' "

Matt Hill nodded bluntly. "All those grandfathers and great-grandfathers who were so fucking heroic. Maybe they knew what they were fighting for—who knows?"

"But if you say that the man who saw combat is the real authority, if you believe that, then you condemn people like poor Dr. Westphall to spend their lives making up for the fact that they weren't in it. He'll have to kill himself trying to even the score."

"That's not the only reason he's killing himself." He lay back on the bed and covered his eyes. "It's funny, really . . . God, is it funny . . . if he only knew what yo-yo's we were!"

"What do you mean?"

"Shit, half the time in Nam we didn't know what we were doing. Where we were or what we were doing."

He was quiet for a while, then he said, "David would probably have been a lifer."

"Why? That's easy to say. And if you say it, you don't have to be sorry he died."

He gave me a wry look. "I wonder what he was like? I mean, did he smoke dope? He was a fool if he didn't; it was so good over there." He walked up and down in front of me.

I laughed, and so did he, and I felt we were friends. At the same time, I had an urge to stick out my foot and trip him.

"He drank beer. In one of his letters he talked about dope. Said it existed, but that he hadn't been able to catch anyone smoking. So I guess he didn't. He wrote to Doug that he didn't need drugs because he had such vivid experiences in his head."

"Women?"

"In Vietnam, I don't know. I think he was more involved with dyeing his packs with India ink and sorting out the equipment he ordered from Gerry's in Colorado than he was with whores. I don't know why he got divorced."

"He'd already been in once. The Corps doesn't exactly prepare you for a healthy relationship with a woman. You talk about surviving. Well, surviving isn't necessarily loving." He sounded bitter. He bent, picked up the candle, and turned it around and around on his palm. "Anyway, what happened?"

Doug: I went to David's graduation at Quantico. It was an ornate military ceremony with typical rah-rah speeches. We each had a car and we loaded them up with his stuff. The South Korean boy he sponsored took pictures of him in the parking lot. On the way to the ranch we stopped at a restaurant and he ordered a hamburger and a malt. He wasn't pleased with the way the malt was made and he said someone should shoot the person who made it. He said it in a way that sounded almost serious. I said, "God, I don't believe you exist." It upset him terribly; he said, "You should never say that to anyone." I regret some of the things I said to him.

I have chastised myself for not going to Vietnam. Maybe I should have gone. Maybe I should have died instead of David.

He did better in school. He was more capable, more intelligent and dynamic. If I had been killed, he probably would have done far more for my memory and for the chapel than I have.

Matt Hill grimaced. "Poor fucker."

Jeanne: When David came home he always said, "Greetings, everyone!" This time he seemed kind of apprehensive, but he came home like any other time. In December he had come home for about a week. He had sold his furniture at school and most of his books. He told me about the pictures they showed at training camp of beaches before and after invasions in World War II. Water filled with blood and things like that. When he talked about those pictures, he'd get tears in his eyes.

He thought those little people shouldn't be overrun by Communists. He thought he should help as much as one person could.

We've had correspondence from people saying you shouldn't teach your children to fight. Who's going to defend the country if we're invaded? Those big, fat, creampuff daddies that run the country? Of course, no one wants their children to fight!

David and Victor took one hike together and David went alone to Wheeler Peak. I think he had a foreboding of what the future would be.

VICTOR: At the ranch David went cross-country to the base of Wheeler Peak—about thirteen miles of very rough terrain—in two days. He probably wanted to prove to himself that he was a Marine physically fit to lead Marines.

DOUG: There was quite a bit of tension at the ranch before David left—between him and Dad, I mean. I had to leave to go to Indiana University. I remember saying good-bye to him. He was due to go to California for overseas orientation to go to Vietnam. It was hard to say good-bye—I knew he was going to severe danger. I said, "Keep your head up while you're keeping it down." He kind of smiled, and shook my hand. My parents went in the house and I drove down the road. He stood outside the house on the hill and waved to me a long time. I remember him that way a lot.

JEANNE: We didn't take him to Albuquerque to the plane. His cousin in Albuquerque took him to the plane. She said she cried because she knew she would never see him again. I took

him to the bus in Taos. Victor didn't even come, he was so
busy with the golf course at the ranch. I remember David had
a seabag and a val-pack, he was wearing slacks and a button-
down shirt. I waited for the bus to leave.

The Continental Trailways bus dwarfs the Taos terminal.
There is barely enough room for it to groan in between the
mud-stained stucco, dirty turquoise-trimmed station, and
Harold Auto Supply next door. Passengers get their first
whiff of the town on clouds of Colonel Sanders, a straight-
ahead view of an abandoned shack in back. Inside the station
is a rundown desk, a tired Spanish attendant, an old candy
bar machine and, on the wall, a faded map of Continental
bus routes. Outside is the rutted road.

Dear Mom and Dad,   Feb 3, 1968

The day before yesterday Lt Stick's platoon was attacked
by two battalions. At Basic School he did 92 push-ups and I
did 93. His platoon killed 112 so we're gunning for 113. The
stresses and strains over here don't bother me much, but
things like my W-2 form do, so I'm sending you mine.

David and Doug corresponded. In general, the letters
from Vietnam glowed with a sense of purpose and exhilaration in the face of hardship.

Dear Doug,
. . . The next day we moved a little further down the
valley then turned in an arc to retrace our steps. The monsoon
had been late up to now, but this day it rained in torrents. The
jungle and the rice paddy we'd been wading around in wasn't

affected much, but waist-deep streams we'd waded coming out were now impassable swamps 300 yards wide. I was put in the point now, with instructions to hurry toward what was a likely crossing on the map in hopes that it hadn't risen too much.

Almost immediately we discovered tracks, obviously too small to have been Occidentals. The scout read them as a mixture of VC and NVA. There was no way I could make any time and check every possible ambush, so I sent a double point as far ahead as practicable and kept everyone widely dispersed. We all expected to be hit any minute as fresh tracks were discovered. There was sniper fire at the rear of the column and this heightened the tension. But we reached the river without incident. It was now impassable. We were cut off from our base and Capt. W. requested a helicopter evacuation with priority for 30 cases of immersion foot many of which had begun to bleed because of the constant water. We were all in sad shape now. I know that at one point, my feet about to crack open, my stomach knotted by hunger and diarrhea, my back feeling like a mirror made of nerves shattered in a million pieces by my flack jacket, pack, and extra mortars and machine gun ammo, my hands a mass of hamburger from thorn cuts, and my face a mass of welts from mosquitoes, I desired greatly to throw down everything, slump into the water of the paddy, and sob. I remember a captain, an aviator, who, observing a group of grunts toasting the infantry in a DC bar, said, "You damned infantry think you're the only people who exist." You're damned right we do.

"Doug believes that, as the war went on, David began to change. In February, 1968, he wrote:

'We're tied to a series of bases, exactly like the French were, with no one, not even one company in this whole division, as nearly as I can tell, left for a blocking force. As soon as the sun goes down, as many gooks as take a notion can walk in between the bases anywhere they want to. Two things are supposed to bring the whole project to fruition: 1) sophisticated surveillance devices will be installed in depth 2) the ARVNs will take over the bases, freeing U.S. forces for maneuver. From here it's most obvious that neither of these two things are, or will for months, if not a year—years—take place. So . . . we're no smarter than the French.'

"Doug says that, whatever David's outrage at the war was, whatever attracted him to the Marines might have overcome it. You know the Marines' saying, 'The only way you can hurt is to die.' Doug thinks David would have been a good leader. He had integrity and devotion to the people under him." Doug believes that, possibly, unconsciously, David wanted to be a decent father to the people under him, to make up for what he didn't have.

"David wrote to Doug in 1969, three months before he died:

'My morale is pretty good, and after all these years—all the adventure I've been through right here inside my own brain—I've finally reached a state in which I can manipulate my mental equilibrium so as to be never actively happy or unhappy, but instead, which is best, constantly pleasantly contented.

Not even our commander can upset me; not even my PFCs and NCOs who, in their own way are as bad as the Colonel, can ruffle me. I'm my own worst enemy, and I approach knowing myself, so how can anyone hurt me?'

"He had numbed himself; he might have gone on, like that, for years."

Matt Hill looked at me. "Hey, there's something I've been meaning to ask you."

"Okay."

"Does this story have an end?"

"You mean like in the movies?"

"Yeah, a happy ending."

"Sure. David Westphall comes back to life, kills the malt maker, and from then on all milk shakes in the country are delicious."

"You're a weird lady."

I laughed hollowly. "Want me to go on?"

He nodded, hunched his shoulders up, and swung his face back toward the fire.

"Jeanne told me the story: 'It was a Monday. Victor had gone up to the golf course on the tractor. There were two Marine officers coming toward him; he didn't pay attention to them really. But they came up to him and said, referring, to David, "Victor," as he was known in the Marine Corps. Victor said, "You mean David!" and they thought maybe they'd made a mistake. Then he got in the car with them and came to the house.

'I had washed my hair and had on curlers and some old boy's boots. I looked like something from the Hatfields and the McCoys. Victor grabbed me and said, "David is dead!" I couldn't cry or anything. I was absolutely petrified.

'They came in later and one of them said it was his first time on this assignment. He said he didn't like it, he'd rather be back in Vietnam. They stayed an hour or two. They said we would get a telegram in the morning mail.

'About 5:00 the telegraph operator from Taos came with the telegram. Things were crossed out, a couple of words here and there. It said: *Dead from small arms fire in the body*, then something was X-ed out, then it said *in the head*.

'We couldn't decide about the funeral. Doug was finishing his tests at Indiana. We wanted the Marine Corps to notify him. They said they would try, then called and said they couldn't. We waited a couple of days. And then Victor called him. Doug couldn't believe it, he said maybe it's a false report. We notified some relatives.

'I couldn't sleep. I just tossed about, and got up, and kept wringing my hands.

'Everyone kept calling us. I couldn't stand the phone calls, time after time; I'd always start crying.

'We thought he'd like to be buried in Santa Fe Military Cemetery, east of the highway. We wanted a military funeral but they ended up giving us an air force chaplain. They said they had a chaplain at Sandia for all services. We couldn't understand. They had three or four weeks to arrange it.

'They had said the body would be arriving on a later day than it did. They called on a Thursday evening, said it was there. I wasn't ready. I didn't have any clothes or anything.' "

I continued: "Doug said, 'I was as concerned about the

fact that David wasn't happy when he was alive as I was that he was dead. It was just a perception. He didn't seem overly enthusiastic about anything. Thrilled by anything.

'The casket was flown from Vietnam to Santa Fe and was on display in Albuquerque. The Marine Corps escort officer met us. We went in to see the coffin, but we never saw his body. Maybe we should have insisted, but at times like that you aren't really thinking. My mother saw the casket and ran toward it, stumbled, fell, and sobbed uncontrollably for quite a while.

'Dad tried to comfort her but he was crying at the same time. They always had the flag over the casket. We didn't see the body. Maybe we should have insisted, I don't know.

'The funeral service was there. Relatives came from Wisconsin and Utah, some of David's friends from high school. A lot of friends of the family. At the service the coffin was between the pews and the altar. Dad walked up and kissed the coffin, then Mom did the same, then they sat down quietly.

'The chaplain took some material from the paper David had written, "A Prophet in His Time." David had been interested in Unitarianism, but the service was nondenominational.

'We went from the funeral home to the cemetery at Santa Fe. They had an Honor Guard and a rifle team fired a volley of blanks. There was a bugler, a chaplain, and the escort officer. He had been wounded in Vietnam, so he was sent back to the States, was recuperating, and was due to go back.

'We went back to the ranch. Dad was building the golf course and I helped him.' "

There was more. "After David's death," I said, "Jeanne stayed for a while in Albuquerque with her sister and in motels. She didn't want to live at the ranch. Springer—sixty miles away—was the only place near enough to the chapel where she would live. Doug told me that after the funeral she talked about sensations of levitating in bed, feeling the spirit was leaving her. She saw lights and rays. 'She became very suspicious of people,' he said. 'I tried to discourage her but it didn't do much good.'

"After the funeral the old man went all over the dump at the ranch, looking for the papers David had thrown out. He never found any. He was nervous, lost weight, and had a heart attack.

"Finally, in the spring, Jeanne and Victor sold the ranch. They moved to Springer and had a trailer built in Texas. Victor devoted his life to the chapel. Jeanne said, 'I went to the chapel at first, but I can't go back any more. Maybe everything's all right, but I have a sneaking hunch it isn't.' "

I got up, stood so close to the door I could feel the cold from the snow on my face. "I'm tired." I spoke to the glass. I felt depressed almost beyond feeling. I felt sick, as though I had witnessed an evisceration.

"You know, the sleepier you get, the prettier you get."

I thought, you wouldn't dare say that to me if I wasn't looking away.

I turned, walked around the bed, and kicked at the candle as I passed. It tottered like a slowing top.

He followed me. I thought, now, because I'm acting like a shit, he's going to put his hands on me, but he went on to the back room and the back door. "Come here," he said. The

back room wasn't finished but he showed me very carefully
how to lock the door. "Will you be O.K.?" he asked. I
nodded. He went out; I held the door open a moment,
watching him, almost calling, come back, don't go. He
turned and squinted at me through the slanting snow. Then
he held up his arm and disappeared. I locked the door and
took off my clothes and climbed into the sleeping bag, which
smelled of mildew.

Mice skittered; the wind moaned, stopped, and started
again. It was the hour of the wolf, not far from dawn. My
head swirled—who in hell do you think you are, you're
tampering, meddling, and you shouldn't be here. I wanted
the fire to keep burning, but I was afraid to get up and throw
on a log.

I must have fallen asleep because the next thing I remember is that I was standing at the door looking down at
the road that leads from the ranch to the highway, watching
a truck make its way through the storm. At that hour in that
part of the world people do not drive. I might have looked
down and seen a dragon huffing along. I was afraid the truck
would turn up to the chapel. I began to dress, plotting
escape. But the truck turned onto the highway and its lights
faded around a bend. I got back into the bag, bunched
my sweater into a ball, and held on to it.

I drifted, observing the fight between fatigue and fear.
Suddenly the room was extremely cold. I got up and walked
toward the bathroom, thinking a window might have blown
open. Instead, the door to the back room was wide open.
The door I had locked. The door I had been taught to lock.
Light from the room illuminated the snow. There were no

tracks. I closed it, making sure again that it was locked. My hand was as cold as the ocean floor.

I sat like a sentry, propped against the end of the couch inside the bag, and stared outside. I felt as though I had forgotten how to blink. The sky turned watery gray and it seemed to stay that way for a long time. The mountain, beyond Angel Fire, grew distinct, looked insanely alive with the sun climbing behind it. Slowly the sky turned silver and blackbirds swooped in great swarms across the valley. My eyes were riveted to the brightest spot above the mountain and an energy came at me, filling me with a force I knew I didn't have. I couldn't move. Viselike tension gripped me until I thought I would scream or throw myself off the bed, and, then, slowly, like melted gold, the sun poured itself up over the rim of the mountain, moving fast until it lay there in the bluing sky. The valley, the chapel, and I fell into relief.

The old man walked through the door.

Nine

I watched him stoke the fire, put water on to boil. My bones felt wet, as though I had run too far, or been drunk for days. I felt lonely and nauseated. I knew there were questions I would never ask him. My wrists tingled, the way they did once just before I fainted. He got out the Maxwell Instant and poured boiling water over the coffee, dropped packets of sugar into each cup.

"Breakfast," he said.

We sat at the table and stared at our cups until the steam subsided. His face was streaked with fatigue. Once in a while, after a sip, he touched his cheek with his worn hand. He asked if I had slept well and I lied. The coffee burned my tongue and I felt dizzy. I was about to make the couch-bed, but before I could get up he was there, rolling the sleeping bag, folding the couch into its daytime shape. His pants bagged about him, but he went about his tasks with determination. Even at daybreak, his energy was formidable.

He sat down again, leaned toward me with a look of tremendous sorrow. "I've been wanting to ask you something, ever since you went to see Sergeant McKinney."

Some time ago I had visited a retired Marine Sergeant who had been in the ambush in which David Westphall was killed. I had wanted to know more about David and about the circumstances in which he died.

"I had a dream," the old man said, "about David's death."

He touched his cheek in the place he had touched it before. "Early only morning not long ago—it was about 4:30—I saw David. He was lying in the dirt and natural growth as he was found on the morning of May 23, 1968. I could see the right side of his face and his right hand standing out as in a Rembrandt painting. The flesh tones were quite brown. From what you learned from Sergeant McKinney, would I have seen his right hand and the right side of his face relatively unscarred?"

I was tempted to tell him that his vision was accurate, that, indeed, he would have seen that side of David's hand and face, but I had to say that McKinney did not tell me those details. He nodded, and drew back into himself.

After a while he sighed. "Sometimes I feel so utterly inadequate. There are so many problems with the chapel. Some of the stereo equipment was stolen and I have had to install a new security system. Money dribbles in and I can no longer meet all the expenses. There have been quite a few visitors, but not as many as in past years. Still, you see, I never cease trying. Doug has been a rock for me to lean upon, but he has his own problems. David's inscriptions in the chapel are a litany which I have repeated daily when the going was rough and I needed a source of inner strength. I do not believe I could have drawn that strength from my personal resources."

I was planning to visit his wife in the afternoon, and I asked him how she was.

"She continues the same. She hasn't been away from the house for months. A while ago some of her relatives were here from Wisconsin, that is, they came to Albuquerque. They took the stand that if they came that far, she should come to Albuquerque to see them. She cried to think that they had so little understanding of her reasons for not doing so. Those reasons are very real to her. I do not know when, if ever, it will change; all I know is that she is reasonably content with her home and her garden, and I ask for no more."

Although it had stopped snowing, I had the sense that snow was piling up outside the boarded-up windows, pressing in against the glass doors. Morning seemed merely a continuation of night.

I asked him if there was any way of getting more money to keep the chapel going. He got up and rustled through a file of papers and thrust at me a letter he had written to Senator Mondale, in 1973, in response to an appeal for financial aid to NCEC:

> The easiest approach for me would be to eke out an amount from an already tight budget for that purpose. There are compelling reasons why I shall not do that.
>
> If you will examine the financial statement in the enclosed

brochure about the Vietnam Veterans Memorial Chapel, you will see that my family and myself have borne, and continue to bear, most of the financial burden. In addition, my personal labors during the past five years in constructing the chapel have been, in numerous ways, comparable to those of Michelangelo in the Sistine Chapel.

One government official once asked: "What's his angle— what does he have to gain? Nobody does anything like that anymore." There is no angle—only a gift to mankind motivated by the philosophy: "We who must will do what we must to encourage mankind to preserve rather than to destroy."

Many thousands have visited the chapel and there have been small contributions, but the wealthy and the important (important in the common usage of the term) have remained away in droves. The chapel is known to millions and in ways has been the conscience of our nation, yet that nation continues to allow one man who is no longer young to carry on the onerous burden of completing construction and somehow creating an endowment for the only substantial memorial to Vietnam veterans in this world.

The letter lay in his bruised hands. His eyes gleamed like a fighter's. He folded it and put it away.

He and Doug had thrown their immeasurable energies into an effort to bring the chapel to the attention of all the families—the next of kin—of men who died in Vietnam. They had launched a campaign in their own fashion—they called it the NOK Inquiry. It had all the fervor of a crusade, the zeal of a mission. It turned into a safari of words. They composed, typed, mimeographed, xeroxed, stamped, addressed, licked, and mailed; they waited, received, opened, answered, and filed. They lived in a maze of letters which piled up in the mobile home in Springer.

They corresponded with agencies, groups, cemeteries, organizations, clubs, individuals, with the deputy assistant secretary of defense, the National Personnel Records in St. Louis. They wrote to every adjutant general in every state in the United States. Some of the states sent the names of the next of kin (NOK);most of them did not. Some states wrote that they did not have the lists anymore; some said they didn't give out such information.

What do the secretaries on their swivel chairs think when they read these letters—these voices stuffed in envelopes that come from the plains, the towns, the mountains; come like late night calls to radio shows; come from folk we call the backbone, or the lunatics; come making the dialogue of democracy? What do they think when they type the answers and then stand, waiting for the dignitaries to sign them?

I suppose the old man dreamed of thousands of photographs of dead soldiers pouring into his postbox, of thousands of markers lying on the ground outside the chapel. There might have been speeches, dignitaries, and congratulations, and the media with its contraptions. The bereaved might have come to shed a tear, pause and wonder how such a place had sprung up in the wilderness, and to thank him. Instead, very little happened, and the NOK Inquiry was, bit by bit, abandoned.

Funds grew shorter. Doug went off to try his staying power at various jobs and schools, and the old man's energy for the chapel lessened. In 1974 they decided to try to interest the government in taking the chapel as a national monument to all veterans of Vietnam. Again, labyrinthine correspondence began. They wrote a lengthy "justification for offering the memorial to the federal government" which included their philosophy regarding memorials:

"With the exception of memorials such as those in Europe which are associated with World War II concentration camps, war memorials have not been consecrated primarily to stimulate a yearning for peace or a repugnance to armed conflict. Instead they have principally attempted to honor men who fought with valor, and who in one way or another paid a high price for their convictions and for those of their society. To honor men for this reason is a totally natural and desirable human motivation. It is an impulse which will and should develop regardless of what risk there may be that succeeding generations will ignore or misuse the memorialization which results. . . .

"The fault is not with the concept or the actual structures. The fault is with societies which do not make use of the beneficial symbolism inherent in memorials. . . .

"The Vietnam war was a disastrous and tragic mistake for which the American people must bear significant responsibility. . . .

"Vietnam veterans should be formally honored by the creation of a national Vietnam veterans memorial. The Federal government has not sufficiently honored those same individuals whom its decisions committed to a decade of mortal combat. . . .

"The Vietnam Veterans Chapel is being offered to the federal government as the national Vietnam veterans memorial which is so demonstrably needed. The offer is being made not only because of the conviction that there should be a federal memorial, but also because the founders have made financial sacrifices for six years and no longer have personal financial resources great enough to effectively perpetuate the memorial. . . . The chapel is worth at least $100,000. . . .

"The chapel is imbued with a unique spirit since its conception, construction, and financial and moral support have stemmed primarily from next of kin of Vietnam War Dead. This spirit results not only from the nature of its origin, but also from the aesthetic appeal of the structural design and from the Chapel's peaceful and magnificent environs. The uniqueness of this memorial could, in fact, not be duplicated even with the expenditure of hundreds of thousands of taxpayers' dollars. . . .

"If the federal government is unwilling to accept the proposed gift, it will have failed to make a noble and moral choice, and it will have failed to take advantage of an opportunity with numerous practical benefits. Most regrettably it will have added but one more tragic chapter to the Vietnam chronology."

Following this came a description of the chapel and its setting, quotes from David's poetry, an outline of future projects, a statement of finances and construction history:

"Dr. Victor Westphall agreed to perform certain portions of the Chapel construction including excavation for the footings and other earth moving. . . . Dr. Westphall supervised much of this construction and performed a great deal of labor as well, and from August 1969 to the present date has done all the supervising and the vast majority of the labor needed to complete the project to the point of being functional. . . .

"As was always the case during the construction, Dr. Westphall was severely hampered by lack of funds, lack of volunteer labor and by inclement winter weather. . . .

"One of the major administrative projects undertaken by Dr. Victor Westphall was the attempt during 1968 and 1969 to secure financial assistance for Chapel construction and perpetuity. Formal applications were made to a wide variety of foundations in an attempt to secure this assistance. Not one of the great and magnanimous institutions applied to consider the Chapel worthy of its support. . . .

"The founders of the Chapel have diligently attempted to make all next of kin of Vietnam War dead aware of the existence of the Chapel. Many next of kin know of the Chapel and have become involved with it, but financial limitations have limited the extent to which publicizing could be attempted. In addition, federal and state laws and policies have severely restricted the number of next of kin which the founders have been able to contact. . . ."

They requested that New Mexico's Congressional delegation propose to Congress legislation which would give the Chapel status as a national Vietnam War memorial under the auspices of the National Park Services.

Correspondence ensued. Months passed. Senator Domenici contacted the American Battle Monuments Commission and the National Park Service. Representative Manuel Lujan introduced the bill, and they waited. In 1975 they were still waiting and writing. There had come to be an expectancy in the old man's voice, and I wondered if he wanted it to be that way.

He got up again and went to his file. "I wonder if you've ever seen this letter. . . . You see, there has been some response from very high places."

THE WHITE HOUSE
WASHINGTON

The Western White House
San Clemente

Dear Mr. Westphall: July 15, 1971

Recently, I read a news account describing the chapel you built to honor the memory of your son and his twelve fellow Marines ambushed in Vietnam three years ago. Your labor of love is far more than the sheer building of a monument; it is a symbol of the love which all fathers have for their sons.

It is written "'tis a happy thing to be the father unto many sons." You have indeed become the father of thirteen brave sons who gave their lives for their country and for freedom. In honoring their sacrifice, you honor the sacrifice of all those who through the history of our Nation have died in order that we may live in peace and with liberty.

With my best wishes,

                              Sincerely,
                              RICHARD NIXON

Two men of the same generation, corresponding.

I mumbled something and handed it back to him. He told me that he was busy working on the book dealing with the history of New Mexican land grants. He made us each a fresh cup of coffee and, when he sat down, he touched his face again. He told me that he had had a toothache for nearly a year. Expensive and complicated dentistry had been to no avail. Still, he continued to run every day and considered it a central feature of his life.

"I began running after David died. I continue it regularly, in spite of the tooth and the other pain," he pointed at his chest. "My tooth condition seems to be an infection from the extraction. In a way I hope it is that rather than some other exotic type of nerve condition. I don't know, but I do know that it is worsened by mental effort and mental stress. Perhaps under the circumstances, it is only human that I try to avoid loading myself in that regard any more than I have to. I have taken on many extra burdens in the past half-dozen years without complaining." He stopped and peered out in the direction of the chapel. His eyes had grown moist and he blinked at the daylight.

"I hope that I'm not complaining, only explaining, but right now it is very much of an effort for me to take on more than my land grant book. I don't want to fall apart completely, and I have the feeling that I could under certain conditions."

I wanted to say something comforting, but I felt trapped in his trap. I thought of *The Immortalist* by Alan Harrington and his words, "The fear of being reduced . . . almost seems to have a life of its own inside one's being." He got up and took the cups to the sink and began to rinse them out.

The sun invaded the hut and I said that I was going for a walk.

Instead, I ran down the hillside, stumbled along a mile of frozen mud ruts, and nearly fell up the steps of the ranch house. "Matt," I muttered to an unshaven, unfamiliar face, "Matt Hill. Where is he?"

He was dressed in a work shirt and the same jeans. He looked haggard. It didn't occur to me that he hadn't been to bed. We walked up behind the ranch in snow that lay under the enormous pines. I told him about the truck and the door and the night. He looked at my face and a glacier formed in his eyes.

"It's all right," I said. "It's over now."

We squatted and looked out over the sparkling valley. The chapel looked like a ship marooned on an iceberg.

"Well," he spoke so quietly I had to pull my scarf back to hear, "you did what you set out to do."

He scooped up some snow, molded a ball, and threw it downhill. It rolled along and stuck on the white crust. He threw another one straight at it and they burst into shards which skittered downwards, etching snow balloons on thin strings in their wake. Then he blew on his bare hands.

I felt my eyes fill with a smile. Sometimes, when a man does something I wouldn't do, I feel threatened, or left out, or disgusted. I recall sitting on sand watching men race into powerful surf, feeling cowardly, resenting the hearty calls to come on in, the beckoning like fins. But rough surf scares me; throwing snowballs at snowballs doesn't. It's just something I wouldn't think of doing. It says: I'm a man; I used to be a boy; it's what I like to do, like skipping stones, or disemboweling telephones, or peeing off the side of a sail-boat. I don't know if New Women are supposed to try those things, too, or if we're supposed to talk men out of doing them. I won't do either because, even though I often think of men as sinister salesmen knocking at my door, I am still seduced by the difference in the way we see things.

At times I am enthralled by what is called maleness, which is that way of doing things, seeing and manipulating things which is different from mine. I marvel at my son, planted firmly on a basketball court, bouncing a ball half his size and throwing it at a basket ten times his height; I like the way grown men step aside for him to take his turn, passing on tradition. It was that boy–man combination that seemed irresistible when Matt Hill threw the snowball, then deftly smashed it with another one.

It does matter to me that a man know how to throw, that he stand straight. I think the Marlboro Man is as silly as a Barbie Doll, but if he rode up outside my kitchen window, I'd find a reason to go outside.

I'm afraid that, deep down, I have more respect for a man who has been through some kind of war than for one who hasn't. I have asked other women about this and, mostly, they disagree, but I am suspicious of them. But how can it be? I am a peace lover, an antiwar freak, a protester, a part-time pacifist. Can you love the soldier and despise the war? If I feel this way, then what hope is there for peace?

In Jean Anouilh's play, *Tiger at the Gates*, the tiger snoozes, biding his time, in peace. Hector comes back from battle to Andromache who is going to have his child. He tells her that war is finished; she says it will come again. They talk

about their child whom Andromache believes will be a son.
"It's because he is you, that I'm so afraid. . . . If you love
war, he will love it. . . . Admit, sometimes you love it.
. . . men do love it."

What is this resignation? Is it only resignation, or is it
partly attraction? If we force men to say they love it, we can
go on blaming them forever. Does this subservience to war
make it happen? Do we women really love it, too?

Hector admits: "But sometimes, on certain mornings, you
get up from the ground feeling lighter, astonished, altered.
Your whole body, and the armor on your back, have a
different weight; they seem to be made of a different metal.
You are invulnerable. A tenderness comes over you, sub-
merging you, a kind of tenderness of battle."

Part of me thrills to Hector's words, even though I am
dumbfounded at the ludicrous nature of men dressed in
costumes with little markings, weighted down with gear. I
am dismayed by men flying planes which make them feel
superior to birds, shooting at one another as though life were
an imitation of dreams, creating missions and patrols and
plans, like the CIA men in their masks, running speedy
boats to Cuba. My son jumps out at me, commando-style,
from behind doors and corners, unaware that, before he
knows it, it will no longer be a game. I scorn all this, but I
have been trained, somehow, to respect it, too. I am amazed
at the brute force, the stamina, the organization and conviction that go into night patrols, radar traps, battle plans; at the
sheer willpower it takes to move the war machine around
the world. I grew up thinking that war was not my realm.
But now that I want to fix my own car, cut wood, and pay my

way, must I consider it too? It is tempting to say, it's too
ridiculous to consider, but it was mostly women, I have
heard, who brought down the Bastille.

So I am ironic with Andromache, but I am drawn to
Hector because he is a warrior. The difference creates the
tension that prowls between a man and a woman. That
difference which Andromache spoke of when she said,
"Whether the marriage is true or false, the marriage portion
is the same: elemental discord . . . there is no tranquility
for lovers."

Would things change if we were neutered, or truly bisex-
ual? Will peace come only by way of terrible androgyny? Is
it true that a woman's picture in a man's wallet will make him
a better killer? Will women always follow the sound, the
sight of combat boots? And will we old romantics be war-
mongers, then, in our secret hearts?

Matt Hill threw another snowball and then stood in a
smooth swift action. His hand dropped in front of my face,
offering me help. I saw my hand go out to take his, and I
stood beside him, stomping my feet. We stood as though we
were stuck. I was so happy to hold his hand that I didn't care
if I froze. Finally, he pulled me to walk higher, up the hill.
The inside of my nose burned from the cold and my heart
thumped from the altitude, and from his hand.

We stopped in a meadow. The chapel lay below us, shorn
of its nighttime power. Down at the ranch the old man
wrestled with a huge machine. I could feel Matt's jacket
through mine. The mountains looked grim in the whitish
air. "Look," I pointed at them, "how ugly they are."

"You know," he laughed, "you need to put on some skis

and forget about everything for a while."

"I'd probably kill myself."

He stared at me and I thought he was going to kiss me. I felt shy, so I asked if he thought I was strange. "A little, I guess, but I like you. I know what you mean about skiing. Sometimes it comes in my head that I'm skiing, fast, in powder, and I aim, on purpose, straight for a tree. That's it, just that. The end of the tracks. I don't know what it comes from. I've never had an accident."

We began to walk again and I stumbled on a log half–hidden by snow. He steadied me and, for the first time since I arrived, I felt safe.

"What'd you do for entertainment the year you lived here?" he asked.

"Went to California."

"Good dope in California." His eyes slanted at me and I saw the Pacific light in them, the long, long waves that come in out of the calm, and the slow afternoon sky sliced into ribbons by missile stripes. You don't care about the missiles, though; you don't care at all, your insides full of cashews and your nose stuffed with the quinine scent of cocaine. "I like California," he said. "Strangers say hello."

"Do you remember how the surfers look? Like black sea birds, waiting out there, and when they walk home in the evening their eyes are empty, as though they'd got everything they needed during the day."

"I remember," he said.

"Where were you?"

"Camp Pendleton."

"That's where I was!"

"You must have been something in boot camp."

I turned down the corners of my mouth which I do, sometimes, instead of laughing. I started doing it in the days when I copied every motion of Jeanne Moreau. I like it when a man makes me laugh; it's a caress, it's being halfway there.

We were quiet, trudging. I remembered getting on the train at Lamy, the little station outside Santa Fe, and heading west in the afternoon. I perched up in the dome car, watched the desert fall behind as we hurtled toward the setting sun. Suddenly the terrain looked familiar. I hung at the window, my heart stuck in my throat, and there it was—the trailer on the edge of Springer, the little putting green, and the redwood stoop. I watched until it slipped behind a bend in the tracks. I imagined I was on a ship, leaving the last bit of American land. I wanted to reach out and touch something, before we passed on.

After awhile there were stars over the desert and I was sleepy, my head full of old songs—tumbleweed, coyote, winding sheet, corral. I thought about what it must have been like to cross in a wagon, beset by everything but the tides. A description in Dr. Westphall's book on Catron, the governor of New Mexico, came back to me: "The (wagon) train traveled about twenty-two miles a day and took three days to pass through the (buffalo) herd. . . . The whole earth seemed to contain nothing but buffaloes, and a very little wagon train drawn by frightened and snorting mules." There is no way you can sit on a train and imagine what it is like to be in a wagon.

Around me in the dome car were older women with wide

bottoms and matching pants suits. They had struck up conversations about their trips, their grandchildren, and their
kidneys. It seemed cozy, the way their lives overlapped.
Once in a while one of them reached into her white vinyl
bag, took out a tiny atomizer, and sprayed her throat with
Lavoris. I thought, they're a generation closer than I to the
wagon.

In the morning we were running parallel to the San
Bernadino Mountains. Snow gleamed on their peaks and, on
either side of the tracks, were rows of stucco houses. One of
them was pale ochre and covered with spangles—water-
shiny and surreal in the early light. Then we passed an old
wooden bevelled-siding house—East Coast gray. A woman
stood in the small yard in a flowered housecoat, her hair
looped in large pink curlers. She made me feel guilty the
way she was standing there, motionless, watching us go by.

Surrounding the houses was the primary thing—growth.
Citrus and palm, eucalyptus, laurel, pine, and cypress.
Groves and gardens and nurseries—things catapulting into
bigness. And the shocking green, green ground. After New
Mexico the green looked degenerate. Trees lining mobile
home courts showered shade down on corrugated metal
roofs. But they didn't grow near the junk plants where cars,
crushed flat, lay in high tidy piles.

We moved in on white and gray, power-wired Los
Angeles. Airplanes circled and sunlight ground against the
tops of thousands of cars in their parking lots. I put on my
dark glasses. When we got off, I had to gasp for air in the
smog, and I stood in the elegant station feeling lost, my eyes
weeping in the city they say delineates the future.

On the freeway I turned the radio up to top volume and drove faster than I ever had in my life. I leaned one arm on the open rented window and wished that I were blonde. It wasn't hard to get to Oceanside; all I needed was an exit number, not even a sense of the ocean. The town looked like an elongated shopping center. It was as though the United States Marine Corps had placed an attenuated green stamp on the shoreline. I stopped at a filling station to ask my way to the Mission Bowl where Sergeant Tom McKinney had said he would meet me.

I tugged at Matt Hill's hand. "Did you ever go to the Mission Bowl?"

"Jesus! What were you doing there?"

"I met someone there."

He shook his head and looked disgusted. I said, "Lots of women with beehive hairdos and slacks and men in uniform."

"Yup."

What I remember most about the Mission Bowl is that it smelled more like a bowling alley than any other bowling alley I had ever been in. That may have been because it had so many lanes, lane after gleaming lane alive with that seductive sound of falling pins, the metallic clack of the pin-setting machine. And the smell—that particular mix of sweat, bowling shoes, beer, and cigarette smoke. It's the most American smell I know. I can conjure it at will, the way men who fought in Vietnam say they can recall the smell of rotten fish cooking, the way people who have lived in New Mexico remember the scent of burning piñon.

Matt Hill said, "Women whose husbands were overseas

used to hang out there till they found someone to take them home. It wasn't hard. There were lots of horny guys around."

"Did you?"

"I wanted to. I really did. I used to plan it out, I even practiced what I would say. But I never could. I was chicken, or something. I never did."

"What did you do?"

"Drank beer, bowled. Got in fights. Went to Tijuana. There was the Mission Bowl during the week and Tijuana on the weekends. Guys used to go down there and drink, and screw, and do drugs. But you know the thing that hit me the most? Guys would come back from Tijuana and say they'd fallen in love. These 250–pound guys getting ready to blow off dinks' heads would go down there and pick a real young whore and they'd come back and say they were in love. It happened in Nam, too. Maybe they were in love. It used to blow my mind. Sometimes I used to wish I was like them. You know? Fall in love with someone you couldn't *speak* to . . . they used to talk about how they were going to go back and marry them!"

He dropped my hand and walked away from me. His feet left wet holes in the snow and the mud glinted up at the sky. His words left a hopelessness in the air which I caught, like a germ. I trudged on behind him until he turned and took my hand again. "So there you were," he said drily, "at the old Mission Bowl."

"I met a man who'd been in the Marines with David Westphall."

I was sorry I had brought it up. I didn't want to tell him

about Oceanside. I didn't see why he needed to hear it. I had made him hear enough.

I had sat at a table at the Mission Bowl and waited for Tom McKinney. He had written to me: "I shall look forward to meeting and talking with you. . . . Lt. Westphall was a fine young man. I shall always remember him."

He had said he'd be wearing a Hawaiian shirt. He had fought in World War II, Korea, and Vietnam and now he was retired and teaching military history in public and military schools. He had, at one point in his career, been in charge of the brig at Oceanside. When he walked in I knew right away that it was he. His graying hair was short, and his face had the kind of lines that look as though they had been carved there. He was trim, he held himself straight, and he walked briskly. His hand was large and its skin was tough.

I followed his spanking clean Volkswagen van that had a Peace sign next to a United States flag stuck on the back. We drove along straight roads, past tidy houses, and lawns, and carports. His house did not stand out. His wife came to the door and smiled up at me. "Welcome to our house," she said. She had a plump cheery face and dark eyes and hair. I wondered if she was part Polynesian, but that may have been because she was wearing a muumuu.

The inside of the house was like a decorated world. A giant console model TV sat on the wall–to–wall carpet. The kitchen was wallpapered and on the wall of the living room was a large rug with a painted peacock which McKinney's daughter had brought back from Germany. Her husband had been stationed there while he was in the army and now they and their baby were living in the house. Her husband worked in a supermarket. The baby was a toddler, named for his grandfather. "He's a mean one, all right," grinned McKinney when the baby was brought in and deposited in his orderly playpen.

On the wall near a picture of Jesus was a photograph of Grandfather Tom with the men in his company, taken in Vietnam. Outside in the garden his work table was covered with plaques, with decals, and with bottles which he cut into lamps. The garden was lined with carefully weeded lettuce, squash, and tomato plants. Knickknacks sat on shelves. In the bathroom mermaids covered the walls and there were foot decals on the bottom of the tub.

Mrs. McKinney showed me photographs taken on their twenty-fifth wedding anniversary. They had said their vows again, and she said she liked it better than their wedding. They had been apart a great many years.

We sat on the couch in the living room and drank Hamms beer. Tom McKinney took out a pocket-size, dark blue, wornout notebook. He opened it and gazed at the lined pages covered with his own handwriting. He spoke so quietly that I had to strain to hear him over the drone of the TV. "I keep in touch with the families." He handed me the notebook. The cover read:

BRAVO COMPANY
4th MARINES

FALLEN COMRADES,

FROM 21 NOV 1967
to 16 NOV 1968

Inside were the addresses of the next of kin. They took up a great many pages.

"Nam was the worst war I was in. One hundred and twenty inches of rain in four months during monsoon. You're either burning up or drowning. You never get dry. Everything molds. Trenches fill up with water. Bunkers cave in. Rats. Leeches, ticks, worms that bury their heads in your flesh and suck your blood.

"I wanted to form a club and meet every year or so and relive old times. There's not many of us left now. You get used to the guys and you look and they're not there. That page in your book is empty; their place is empty. That hurts."

I handed him back his notebook. We sat still in the blather of the evening news.

Mrs. McKinney called us for dinner. In the middle of the linoleum table was a blue plastic flower on a white plastic doily. The kitchen was cheerful and warm. We ate pot roast, mashed potatoes, carrots, and peas. No one talked much, but after coffee McKinney leaned back in his chair and said, "I suppose you'd like to hear about David." I said I would.

"The first time I saw David he was covered with jungle rot, sitting in a corner of a bunk. I had just come into the company. It was raining like hell and he was stripped to the waist, wore muddy boots and a week's beard. He had kind of long reddish hair. Nothing about him told you he was an officer. 'You're in the company?' he wanted to know. 'I'm your new first sergeant,' I said.

"He had been ambushed three days before—eight or nine

killed, twenty-five to thirty wounded, one boy gone crazy, throwing grenades at people.

"David *wanted* to be a Marine officer. He wanted a taste of leading men in combat. He would have stayed in the Marines and would have accepted being a regular.

"David used to talk about his father. I knew his Dad was the sole surviving son in World War II. He talked about his brother, too. He was going back to Eagle Nest on his leave.

"He was hard-working and conscientious. He had a dry sense of humor and he loved to eat. He had the eatingest damn platoon you ever saw. He couldn't drink; he wasn't used to it.

"David always wanted to know why. When we moved to Yankee Station, some of his squad was playing football with no jackets, which was illegal—fourteen or fifteen guys right in the middle with no jackets. I said, 'That's it, run 'em in here, $25 fine each.' He came to CP and said he wondered why they couldn't have recreation!

"He used to question orders and get away with it. Once they wanted all the guys to give money to help the Vietnamese people. The captain said, 'I've been told that is what we're supposed to do.' A lieutenant questioned him and was relieved of duty on the spot. David said, "Can we talk to the one who told you?' and he got away with it."

Mrs. McKinney began to clear the table and we went back to the couch in the living room. The baby played with a teething ring.

"It was 5:30 P.M. We were northwest of Con Thien. The country was rolling, we were going downhill toward the Ben

Hai River. The roads were dry and dusty, there was no water, it was 100 degrees in the shade. It's never cool till 11:00 P.M. and, even then, it's just a small change.

"We were heading toward Village Three, one of the old French villes—just some low walls that have been fought over I don't know for how long, and cleared areas where the houses were burnt, and nothing growing. We were 200 yards away from it. There were two long, low mounds in front of it, covered with grass. One was 100 yards long; the other 50 yards. They were high enough to hide men.

"Our lead scouts got over them before the NVA opened fire. There were 75 to 100 of them. They had dug in the back sides of the mounds and they had mortar, machine guns, automatic rifles, two M60 machine guns, one 1919 A4 machine gun, two 60 MM mortars, and a couple of 50 calibres. Our guys were yelling and screaming and hitting the ground. Nobody could say they saw or heard a signal given—just all of a sudden all hell broke loose.

"It was an L-shaped ambush. David was in the first platoon which was in the lead, the center for motion. The second platoon was on the left and back. Third on the right and back. Company CP was behind the first platoon, eighty yards back. We had scouts out. A fire team—four men out front and in the flanks.

"The second platoon brought people up on line real quick, but the first platoon couldn't fire. The guys over the mound were wiped out to start with. The third platoon turned right and went shooting like hell. It was the first time we saw enemy rifles and bayonets running at us; NVA running straight at us. Captain Harris was shot right through the heart. A grenade got the 60 machine gunner. Someone started to yell, 'Corpsman!'

"I don't think the NVA saw the second platoon which moved in on the first and tried to cover them. The NVA got the worst end of it real quick, and all of a sudden, they weren't there anymore. Artillery came in so we all had to pull back. The second and third formed the perimeter and we pulled in everyone we could. There were quite a few wounded and the corpsmen went to work.

"The battalion at Con Thien could see us. We got them on the radio. It occurred to me that we didn't have an officer. We thought we'd lost them all. Then we found out we had an air officer and an artillery officer. The artillery officer took command. David and thirteen others were dead.

"We told the battalion we needed people and air to get the wounded out. The first chopper with four or five wounded took us to Dong Ha to medevac. I went to the company command and pulled the record books on the wounded as they came in. They brought Boyd in. I felt closer to him than any of the young NCOs. His color just told me that man wasn't going to live. He had bottles hanging off him everywhere possible to hang a bottle on a human. He died the next morning.

"It was midnight before the last wounded left. I got a good picture of who wasn't coming back.

"They found sixty NVA bodies. All the American bodies were stripped of helmets and flack jackets. They found American machine guns and artillery. We put our dead on tanks and the rest of B Company swept the area, dug out mounds, and found bodies inside.

"I took every man I had in the rear and when the choppers came in, *we* unloaded our dead. We had to go through and identify them after they were cleaned up.

"Everybody was hit in the front. We had walked right into it.

"Kirkland was shot through the head, five or six times.

"James R. Joshua, the colored boy with the perpetual grin, was dead. It was the first time I knew a colored guy not colored all the way through. His skin was peeled off and under the black it was snow white.

"Captain Harris looked like he had just fallen asleep. He was thirty-six, the oldest man killed.

"David had four or five bullet holes—along the neck, chest, shoulder, below the flack jacket. David had been in Vietnam longer than just about anybody.

"I sent home David's pack. While we were at C2 position, he got an orange pack on a frame. He got Marine Corps green paint and taped the aluminum frame so it couldn't be seen. He was real fond of that pack. He had a canteen for a gallon of water, a hand axe, a machete. He needed two bags for all his stuff. He had all kinds of books. A space blanket. He had more equipment than the law allowed. He was a regular pack rat.

"I sent Dr. Westphall my flag from the Second World War. It was a flag David had wanted."

The lines in Tom McKinney's face looked deeper than before, and his eyes seemed to have folded down over his memories. He went on, almost as though he were talking to himself.

"Guys grow up in Nam. At first they're fresh, all they

know is combat films, they come with brass knuckles and Bowie knives and all that garbage. They're cocky, wear their chin straps up, flack jackets unzipped, shoot their mouths off about how many gooks they're gonna kill. First thing that happens they pick up the language, they say *Nam* and *goin' forward*.

"After they're done at the rear, you take 'em to the helicopter strip. They know the game is for real. They see the guns out of the copters, bullet holes in the copters, nothing but combat equipment. They know the next place they see could be the last place.

"You see the changes: the strap comes down, zipper comes up. These kids all clean and shiny, they get quiet watching the filthy stinking guys coming off the copter. They're thinking, uh oh, there's the veteran. After that, any chance to rest they take; they change real quick. That's when the chain starts. If he lives fourteen months, he goes home a different man.

"Guys wear themselves out emotionally. They think too much about the guys killed and wounded."

He was silent for a while. It was getting late and I thought that I should go. Before I left, I asked him who had been David's friends in Vietnam.

"All of David's best friends are in there," he said, and pointed at the dark blue notebook.

•   •   •

Matt Hill and I slipped and slid downhill, brushing withered sage and frozen camomile. We were moving as though we knew where we were going, holding onto that camaraderie that comes with walking in stride. When we got to the road, Matt stopped to move a large stone that lay in the tire tracks. I watched the way he bent and then straightened. He was a slim man. I thought, we could just keep walking, walking in the memory of that California light, out along the highway, far away.

"There's a bar," he said, "in Eagle Nest. They have draft beer, anything you like, and honest old-fashioned hamburgers. Aren't you hungry?"

I was. Starving. I saw Eagle Nest in my mind: the log cabin bar, motels, the icy lake behind. I saw a scratched table with thick pine legs, and hard chairs; heard Merle Haggard harangue from the fifties juke box.

Our elbows would lean on the table, the beer mugs would empty one by one. Or I might drink vodka, let it slice me in two. Our heads would droop toward each other. We would be two people with moist palms in a bar on a road in a small town in the middle of the day. There would be a swizzle stick—maybe even a cocktail napkin, but a swizzle stick for sure—for me to bite on until I broke it in two, and then played with the parts, placing them in endless X's across the table. The town would be a choice of rooms with double beds and a lake. You cannot see the chapel from the town.

"I'm hungry," I said, "but I promised to go to Springer this afternoon." The old man had left already, and they would be waiting for me.

"You're a real masochist, aren't you?"

"I'm coming back tonight," I said.

He turned slightly away.

I thought he was angry, and I didn't know why. I tried to

humor him by saying that it was nice it had snowed because he would be able to ski.

He said, "I don't think I'll hang around."

"Where will you go?"

"There's lots of mountains."

I put my hand on his arm. "Don't you have to work today?"

"I'm taking off."

"I'll be back by sunset," I said, "then we can go to Eagle Nest. O.K.?"

I had a terrible lump in my throat. I hardly knew him, but all the silly comforting words of parting were rushing through my mind.

With both hands he held my coat by the collar. "I want you to be careful, hear? Very careful."

I promised. And I climbed the hill, got in my car, and drove away.

Ten

In Springer they were waiting for me on the red-wood stoop. The sun had come out and turned the snow to slush. I was careful to scrape my boots before we went inside. The old man went into his study and Jeanne put the kettle on to boil. Instinctively, I looked for the pistol, but it wasn't there. Once I had asked Doug whether he thought she might shoot me. "No," he answered, "but she might think about it after you had gone." He had convinced her to keep the clip separate. "She could shoot someone in the right circumstances," he said.

She sat across from me at the kitchen table and told me that the old man had been crying because their cat had been missing for several days. She frowned, shaking her head, "He gets so upset. . . ." she whispered with a mixture of dismay and disgust, as though she were speaking of an

overly emotional child, "he talks baby talk to that cat. He's
been out calling for her ever since he got home."

The kettle began to hiss. She measured instant coffee into
cups, set the Coffee Mate on the table. Their lives appeared
to be utterly without festivity, and their provisions were
those of a perpetual camping trip. She put six chocolate chip
cookies on a plate. The old man joined us and we went into
the living room. I sat beside her on the couch, facing David's
portrait which hung on the wall.

Jeanne took out a box of photographs. She said that she
had been going through them and thought I might like to see
them. I was glad to, partly because I was curious, partly
because the atmosphere was strained. I sensed that they
both had things to say to me, but that they didn't want to say
them in front of each other. She handed me a picture of
David as a small boy with his father. The striking thing about
the photograph was the father's pose: dressed in an old-
fashioned bathing suit, he knelt with one knee on the
ground, propped the other at right angles to it, and
stretched his arms over his head, supporting the child. His
body looked as if it had been oiled; all of his muscles were
flexed, and bulging. He looked like a model for the Charles
Atlas body-building ads that used to be on the back of comic
books. It was hard to associate the picture with the shrunken
man who sat in the large armchair across the room. I put it
back and took a sip of coffee.

She passed me another one—David in a football shirt with
padded shoulders—a bright face from the fifties. He was
smiling and his neck looked strong, his cheeks well-fed, still
uncontoured by time. There was a light in his eyes, as

though he expected to have fun, to play hard, and to go far. He was handsome, the sort of boy you would choose for your team. I imagine that was the way the old man wanted to remember him. After all, he was his boy, "an extraordinary physical specimen." He had letters in football, track, and wrestling. The old man had raised him the only way he knew how, and now, with his terrible restlessness, he was trying to understand why he had died. And all the while he battled, as he always had, his assailants, which came in the guise of feelings. It was that legacy—stare down your feelings until they shrivel before your eyes—which he had passed on to his boy.

David's hair was short, parted on the side. "He was in high school," Jeanne brushed at his forehead where a wisp of his hair had come loose from the rest.

A line of Erik Erikson's came to my mind: "In mourning we become the lost person *and* we become again the person we were when the relationship was at its prime."

The best time that Jeanne and David had together was when he was small and Victor was away. She had spoken of those days with particular tenderness—days when David had picked flowers and learned to read and surprised the neighbors by talking like a grown-up. They had gone swimming and sledding and there was no one to tell them what to do. She had guarded him as he grew as, today, she guards what he left behind. Her mourning—an affirmation of continuity with the dead—is relentless. The chapel is a travesty in her eyes; only memory commemorates and will not die.

She put the photograph down gently and took up another one: David before Vietnam, thinner but still full-faced, more serious now, but looking out with half a smile. He appeared intelligent and full of determination. He was wearing the pressed hat, shirt, and tie of the Marine Corps uniform, the Corps insignia on his hat and collar, a marksman's medal hanging from his shirt at chest level.

I remembered McKinney's words: "David *wanted* to be a Marine officer. He wanted a taste of leading men in combat."

He looked as though he knew where he was, and though the going was going to be tough, he liked it. He was doing what he had learned to do.

She placed the photograph on the couch between us, and, with a small hesitation, slid another one in beside it. I tried not to show the shock I felt when I saw it. At first I thought it was the face of someone I knew—was it Matt Hill, or someone else? I caught my breath.

"It's the last picture that was taken of him," she said.

He was dressed this time in rumpled, open-necked fatigues and helmet. The only mark on his clothes was V WESTPHALL right above the pocket. His eyes were thinner and tired. His hair had grown out and curled around his ears, his face was thin, and lines ran alongside his mouth, which was closed in a grim line. He had his strap up under his chin.

As often happens in photographs, each eye bore a different expression. His right eye looked straight at the photographer with clarity and a hint of brightness. The left eye was full of hurt and hatred. It was the eye of a man who could kill you.

". . . they change real quick. That's when the chain

starts. If he lives fourteen months, he goes home a different man."

But it was David's overall expression in that picture that has stayed with me. With the exception of that small gleam in his right eye, his face had an expression of hurt and self-taught invulnerability meshed in such a way that he looked like a mummy.

"I've finally reached a state in which I can manipulate my mental equilibrium so as to be never actively happy or unhappy, but instead, which is best, constantly pleasantly contented."

He had attained the goal he had been taught to seek. He had plowed under his emotions and, in their place, cultivated a garden of duties. After years on the gridiron he was finally in the field, and he was well trained to deal with the pain that told him he was alive. "I'm my own worst enemy, and I approach knowing myself, so how can anyone hurt me?"

All across America, fathers stand up and salute the sons who talk that way. Saluting, they approve the proving grounds. They skulk at the sidelines. They are the crowds and the coaches and the corpsmen. When it is time, they run past perimeters, carrying the cure-alls, manning the ambulances.

They are the first to wave when the son goes down like a man.

"The only way you can hurt is to die."

· · ·

There must have been a sound at the door because they

both stood up and walked quickly to the entranceway. I could hear them talking outside. A sleek cat trotted in, looking as though she had feasted on birds. Jeanne followed her, went to the refrigerator, and poured fresh milk into a small bowl. The old man came behind, saying, "Good pussy, pussy, pussy, where you been, naughty cat, we've been worrying about you . . ." His wife made a kind of humming as she set the bowl on the floor. The cat lapped the milk, oblivious to their sounds.

The old man asked if I would like to see his study. We went into the back part of the trailer. The study was an addition he had built; books lined the walls and papers covered his desk. There were filing cabinets and weights for weight lifting. He pulled out a photograph which had appeared in an old issue of *Life* magazine. One half of it was of the chapel, the other half of the old man, in profile, his face lifted toward the sky as though he were praying. He had shown it to me before; I admired it again. He pulled out another picture by the same photographer—himself wrestling in a strong wind with the flag that hangs from the flagpole at the chapel. It looked like a war photo, and he looked as though he had been in a battle.

"It's been a long struggle," he said. "But it seems as though everything in my life has prepared me for the task of working on the chapel. It has been a long and often lonely road."

He took out some charts which explained his running records. I listened while he talked, but I wasn't sure why he was telling me.

"On my sixtieth birthday, October 13, 1973, I celebrated

by setting two new personal running records: 60 yards in 7.6 seconds and 100 yards in 12.7 seconds. Of course I pay a price, but what would life be without continuing to meet challenges? It is a hobby which continues to be a source of personal pleasure and mental relaxation. Last spring I ran ten miles on each of three successive days. This fall I did one and a half miles in 11:10."

He pointed out a large object which lay on a shelf. He explained that he had designed and made it, that it was a vibrator which he could affix to any part of his body, like a yoke and which soothed his aches and pains. The cat had come in behind us and jumped up on his desk chair. He stroked her, "Good pussy, you be good pussy now . . ." He turned with a stricken look. "I talk to her the way I talk to my boys at the chapel. Baby talk, I guess. Jeanne said something about it the other day. I think it bothers her. I said, 'I can't help it; it's my way.' "

We went back to the living room and the afternoon evaporated in small talk. The light grew diffused and we might have been in an Edward Hopper painting, there in the middle of the lonely land, the only sounds beside our voices the whirr of the automatic heater, and, once, the Super Chief flying by. The old man sat in the naugahyde armchair, arms stretched above his head like a steeple. He flexed them when he talked about his chores. His voice grew strident when he said, "If 10 percent of the people in this country did 10 percent of what I do, our problems would be greatly solved." It was as though he were giving us a speech, and we nodded, two women on the couch across from him.

When it was time to go, they came outside with me. The

little putting green had turned to slush. "Listen," he grabbed my arm, "listen to those trucks, night and day, any time of the night or day you hear them."

"The sound bothers him," she said matter-of-factly.

"You can't get away from them." He tightened his jaw and glared in the direction of the highway where the trucks lumbered on past Springer toward Santa Fe, toward Raton.

They waved at me until I was gone.

•   •   •

I drove as though I were running from a grave. I put the old people and the chapel out of my mind, and thought about Matt Hill. The road twisted and straightened; the car careened. I passed through the Cimarron Canyon where aspen and pine climbed the cliffs and, high overhead, the Mayan shapes watched. The wind blew in the canyon. I knew there were fat trout in the stream and silver lichen on the rocks, but I didn't stop. I thought about Matt Hill and I imagined us walking in the glacial light. I thought, we could just keep walking, away from the chapel. On the highway between Eagle Nest and the ranch there are some small log cabins with tarpaper roofs and turquoise window frames. I had always thought that if I got caught in a snow storm, I would stop there. We could leave the chapel, get to the end of the road, turn left, and go there. We could walk. We wouldn't have to say anything, just turn in by the lake at the sign: Thunderbird Motel—Kitchenettes. There would be an old man who would take our money and tell us to go on in; there would be no key.

Outside our cabin there would be an old metal patio chair

with a scallop shell bottom, leaning against the wall under a rusty wind chime. The wood from the woodpile would be wet, so the fire would take a while. The room would bloom with smoke. The lake would cast a glint through the windows and the wind would leak through the chinks between the logs.

I went on imagining:

We sit cross-legged in front of the smoking fire and our eyes fill with tears. We keep our jackets on. I hug my knees, wondering why, every time, it seems so difficult. Every first time seems insurmountable. I always want to run away; I want it to last; I want it to go fast. I want it all. There is the terrible mystery, the awful question of how it will be. I think that I won't move; I'll stay hunched beside the fire all night.

We look at each other's streaming eyes and laugh. It is not at all romantic. Matt Hill reaches into an inner pocket of his jacket, pulls out some papers and some grass, and rolls a joint. "We won't smoke much," he says, "because we haven't eaten." I think it's amazing when someone tells me what I will or won't do. I have been in charge of myself and my children so long that it upsets my balance. When it is right, I like it as much as anything I can imagine.

I take the joint between my thumb and index finger and draw the smoke into my lungs and cough as I exhale. My eyes burn. I give it back to him and our fingers touch in the exchange. Something in me shrinks away.

We smoke silently and then he rubs it out, slips it back into his pocket. The fire has begun to take hold. Matt Hill gets up and opens the window. The aging afternoon light comes in with the sound of the lake. I think I ought to say something. I was brought up thinking I should have something to say on all occasions. But the dope has made me dumb, and I stare at his back as he stares out the window and the fire makes a sound like the crack of a breaking wave.

It seems that he stands at the window a long time. I wonder if he is sorry we came. It's the dope—it hangs up fears, like evil puppets, in your head. In this cabin I forget how precarious it is for him to cross the room. I see only me, myself, tilted at the edge of a gamble, waiting to close my eyes.

I wonder if he knows how small my breasts are. A man once said to me, "Did you know that all men are either tits or ass men?" I said, "I never knew any of the first," and he laughed, and said, "Yours are beautiful," but I didn't believe him. They don't sag, they're just small. I used to mind a great deal. When I was a teen-ager, I stuffed my brassiere with cotton. Now I don't even wear one, but in the cabin room I think of it, and I wonder if he minds.

He seems to have forgotten me. I feel angry; I'm not sure what I gave up by coming here, but it must have been something. He turns and walks toward me, leans down,—the way he did when he picked the stone out of the road,—and lifts me underneath the arms. The zipper of his jacket cuts cold into my cheek.

All the longing of the night and day are in our arms. We stand in the cabin in the room and wrap and unwrap each other—arms around necks, ribs, waists, hips. His hand guides my head into the curve of his neck and holds it there.

He bends me back a little and smiles, "You're tall."

"Too tall?"

"You just fit."

We look at each other's faces. Just as when you push your face close to a mirror, there is no escaping the eyes. I try to see the contours of his face, the lines of his mouth, but his eyes are in the way. There is nothing to say. The silence that comes when you slide over the edge, past the gamble, into darkness, begins between us.

In the room of the cabin there are two old metal beds with a table and a kerosene lamp between them. On the bed there is a yellow chenille spread worn smooth by washing. On the bed there is no privacy and I lose track of my rhythm. We turn over and over as though we were on a hill, and we gasp at each other through our pores and through our clothing. It is always a tremendous question: undressing. Clothes are the last link with the world. If someone rips at my clothes, it seems like an imitation of passion and it makes me cringe. Matt Hill sits up over me and takes off all of his clothes. His skin is darker than I would have suspected, and his arms are larger. I lie dead still, afraid to see, afraid of the hollow place in my center.

"Take off your clothes."

I sit up, feeling that I move in slow motion, pull my sweater over my head and my jeans off my legs. I glance at him furtively, for approval. He looks as though he were staring at a puzzle. He runs his index finger along the scar that divides my stomach. "What happened?"

"A cyst."

He leans down and rubs his lips along the scar. One of my little fingers begins to move by itself—a frantic little motion. I remember that the first time I went to bed with a boy I got a cramp in my toe. I smooth Matt Hill's hair which is soft, like my child's, and I draw his head to my chest. It begins to work—a million pieces falling into place, nerves touching blood touching tears.

Fingers stray and return to one another. It is as though they grow out of each other, leave, like wild birds, flying to all the destined parts, all the woods and swamps and shores, and then return. We stop, his palms spread out on top of mine, for an instant, before he turns me on my side, and I wrap my legs around him, and he pulls me against him in a rhythm that grows rigorous, and unrefined.

In stages I lose touch with my mind. There are times when I never lose it—it stays there, observing, bickering, straying. Only shared sensuality, like matching ribbons, can drive it out; soon there is movement, and no mind. Once in a while, he stops, and I feel his heart battering and I hear our breathing and he waits for me to urge him, and a barrier falls slowly apart in me, until I don't know anymore, or care anymore, until, finally, I wake, brought home to my own sounds.

Outside the window the mountains lie in the remnants of the day. The lake is still as the ocean in summer. Matt Hill lights the kerosene lamp. It smokes a little, flickers, and gives off a bittersweet smell. We can see our shadow, like a large lump, on the ceiling. Our bodies dry, like sand at low tide. Soon it will be time.

I had hardly noticed that I had passed the cabins and the lake. Excitement was on the rampage in my car. It had been a long time since I had wanted to see someone so badly.

Girlish frights afflicted me: did I look all right? What would
we say? Where would we go? Would he like me? What if he
wasn't there? My hands felt knotted to the wheel. I made the
turn off the highway sharply, raced up the rutty road. There
was a light on in the bunkhouse. Smoke from the chimney
was darker than the darkening air. The door opened and
someone stepped out, holding up a hand, as if he meant to
wave.

I got out without closing the door. The unshaven face
came into my headlights. I stopped, full of fear.

"Matt Hill," he said, "he's gone."

"What?" The word came out a shriek.

"He said he's sorry, he's gone."

Eleven

I got to Santa Fe that night and sat in the bar at the old La Fonda Hotel, watching people dance. I went to bed and waited for the cathedral bell to ring in the morning. I drank coffee downstairs, next to an adobe fireplace, and wandered around the town, carrying my pride like a broken egg.

In the plaza Indian women were arranging their jewelry on rugs they spread on the pavement. Their eyes looked damp and avaricious. Their men were probably still sleeping. I wondered if they cared; it was probably better to squat in the plaza than to squat at home. Santa Fe is the only beautiful city in this country, but it looked drab and sad under its sheet of early snow. I stopped in my tracks: he rounded a corner ahead of me, stepped through a doorway in the arcade. I lurched ahead, clutching my shoulder bag, slipping on the wet street, scarcely breathing.

I got to the door of the shop and peered in past racks of Mexicana—shawls, rugs, pots, pottery, earrings, mirrors, toys, and moccasins. He stood at the counter with his back toward me. He was wearing his jeans, his boots, and his hair curled over the collar of his fatigue jacket. The saleswoman was speaking to him. He was buying a gift. It had to be for a woman; it was a shop full of women's things. For me? I wondered crazily. How would he know where to send it? I started toward the door as he turned slightly and I saw that he wore no glasses, that he had no dark mustache, that his nose was long and narrow. He wasn't even the right size. A car passed, churning up slush, and I followed it blindly.

I couldn't understand why it hurt so badly. I walked, talking to myself: why was I mourning something I hadn't even wanted—one night in a room in a cabin? Was it greed, or loneliness, or fear? Would it have kept me from the clutches of the story? Convinced me that I was not an observer on its battlefield? Not a rabbit in an old man's bag of tricks? Not just the recorder of a tragedy, not a name on a roster, not another casualty?

I wanted to kick in a door, or break a window. If Matt Hill had come around the corner I would have spit in his eye. He had behaved badly; he was rude and unfair. I should have known. I had known them before. I stomped off a curb into a puddle, splattering my legs. My feet were wet and cold. I wondered if I was ugly.

Without a plan I went to the herb shop. In the front were pots and pans and kitchen soap. The whole room smelled of sassafras, of camomile, and thyme. The old Spanish man came forward, peering at me from behind his thick glasses.

"You need something?"

I nodded. I hovered before the large glass jars full of roots, spices, and cures. The names were Spanish—malva, yerba buena, chamisa, yerba santa. "I feel bad." I sat down in his peeling chair.

"Where?" He touched his stomach, his throat, his head.

"I don't know." My voice sounded small. "All over. Everywhere."

He bent forward, squinting. His glasses glinted in the overhead light. "All over?"

I nodded, and my mouth began to tremble.

He walked away, pausing in front of his jars, muttering in Spanish, came back with a small paper bag filled with raspberry leaves. He held it in front of me. "You make a tea, leave five or ten minutes, drink, very good, *muy bueno.*"

Raspberry leaves, for cramps, labor pains, and hemorrhaging. He placed it in my hand, patted my shoulder. "*Es bueno,* you be better." "Thank you," came out like a squawk. I clutched the bag. If he said another kind word, I was going to cry. His prescription was perfect, although he couldn't have known what I was suffering from, that I felt rejected and sad, that I was sick to the heart with a plain, old-fashioned, implacable wound.

I paid him and thanked him. His singsong speech trailed me out the door—"You come back again. . . ."

The city bristled with traffic and shoppers. The sun had slipped through the clouds. I felt so terrible that I decided to do something I had avoided for a long time. It couldn't make me feel worse. I headed north, in the direction of the Cemetery.

●   ●   ●

I hadn't gone there before because I had always suspected that I wouldn't have liked David Westphall. I knew that, in order to tell the story, I would have to go there, but I feared, superstitiously, that if I went to his grave, not liking him, his ghost would stalk me. I thought that I should have been sorrier than I was, that I should have felt that his death left a gaping hole in the world. The only time I felt that way was when his mother talked about him, and then I felt sadness for her, for the parents of all dead children. Not for him, or for me.

Since I had begun to tell the story to Matt Hill, however, I had begun to see David in a different light. The story had led me onto cold stones, but I could see, now, a larger landscape. I realized that David was a man who had, essentially, been driven from his home. A letter from Vietnam which his mother had shown me stayed in my mind:

> When I was an enlisted man I swore that if I ever had the chance and authority, the typical, bastardly mess cook would tremble at my approach. Our chow hall was getting more and more fouled up and going from bad to worse. So I volunteered to be the company mess officer, and set about to straighten things out. The head cook, an old gunnery sergeant with twenty years in the service, thought he would buffalo the young punk second lieutenant, but I gave him such a blister-

ing ass-chewing and made so many threats that he found himself standing at attention. Now they tremble when I approach. The mess hall is squared away. Pure pleasure.

But I realized now that he was a man whose life had taught him that such behavior won approval. So I approached the cemetery with mixed feelings.

The gates were open and pine trees dropped small bouquets of showers. Hundreds of white headstones gleamed in the bright sun. In spite of last night's snow, the grass was green. I walked up the road to the office. Inside a man in a tweed jacket sat at a desk. A picture of John Kennedy hung on the wall. I gave David's name and asked how I could find the grave. He handed me a map on which he made an X inside a circle at the appropriate spot. He wrote in 510 after Grave, and, after Section, U. In addition, he gave me the cemetery literature: a sheet of INFORMA-TION CONCERNING PLACING FLOWERS AND WREATHS ON GRAVES IN NATIONAL CEMETERIES and a booklet on the history of the cemetery which ended by saying, "Here at Santa Fe National Cemetery the flag of the United States is proudly flown. Here well-kept grounds and ordered rows of headstones and monuments commemorate the lives and services of those who, each in his own way and according to his talents and abilities, contributed to the growth, development and preservation of this nation. A grateful nation honors those who have served it well."

A fatter pamphlet, INFORMATION COVERING IN-TERMENT IN NATIONAL CEMETERIES, contained in-structions covering all aspects of military burial including headstones, markers and private monuments, eligibility for national cemeteries, interment costs, graveside religious services, viewing of remains at graveside, lowering of burial vaults, and disinterment. One section in particular struck my eye. It was listed under Requirements for Interment and under Public Health Service: "f. *Minor Children* of an eligible service member may be buried in a national cemetery but only in the same grave in which either parent will be or has been interred, if space therein is available. . . . Not more than one gravesite may be used for the interment or future interment of the persons involved in the spouse-parent-child relationship."

I stepped outside and followed the map in the direction of Section U. I glanced at the general information at the bottom of the map:

1. Cemetery *will not* be used as picnic grounds.

2. Visitors *will not* litter the grounds, cut, break, or injure trees, shrubs, or plants, or otherwise conduct themselves in a manner not in keeping with the dignity and the sacredness of the Cemetery.

3. All graves will be decorated during the 24-hour period preceding Memorial Day with small flags, which will be removed immediately after Memorial Day. Flags are *not* permitted on graves at any other time.

Jeanne had wanted to put David's old flag on his grave, but it was forbidden.

I plowed on, past row after row of headstones. My feet left

wet prints on the grass behind me. There was a group of
people in the far eastern corner and I realized that they were
burying someone. It was a small group. They all wore dark
coats and the women wore black veils. I couldn't tell from
where I was, but I thought that they were Spanish.

Suddenly I was in a hurry to find him. I felt lost in a field of
anonymity, bewildered by numbers and unknown names.
Wind caroused in the pines and cars zoomed by on the
highway beyond the perimeter. The sky had cleared to an
impeccable midday blue. I kept track of the numbers, looking for # 510. I went south, then to the right, farther south, a
bit to the left, until I found it.

VICTOR DAVID WESTPHALL III
NEW MEXICO
1ST LIEUTENANT
UNITED STATES MARINE CORPS
VIETNAM
JAN 30 1940
MAY 22 1968

A pink plastic rose was beside the grave in a small con-
tainer sunk in the ground.

I squatted in front of the marker. I was relieved to find it
and I wanted to say something. I wanted to say, I'm sorry for
all the waste, or I'm sorry that you died. I wanted to say that,
perhaps, the world would make up for it in some way. But it
may have been the pity I had for my own life just then, or
maybe it was the cynicism of the times that muted me.

All I could think of was a letter that David had written to

his brother in 1964 after his first tour. Doug was considering going into the Marines.

> I'd like to say that the Marine Corps is the last place to go to solve your problems. You've already had a glimpse at it. And after three or four years you'd end up like the slobs who whine and curse at it. Believe me, I was starting to. The stupid, senseless atmosphere that arises from the sloth and inanity of the Marine Corp's so called leadership, can only end by degrading any intelligent person. If you must go, go as an officer; and even then, I believe, you'd find it stifling. Possibly even in extra measure . . .
>
> So my advice is, use your imagination. Talk it over with someone. Write me a letter if you'd like. Or do something out of the routine or unusual to break away to a fresh way of looking at things. But I don't think the Marine Corps is the answer.
>
> Love,
> David

God makes each of us in many molds.

I remembered Doug's words: "The tragedy of David's life was not that he died, but that his life wasn't happier."

I stood up and looked at David's neighbors. There was Jack Benson, Jr., who served in World War II and José Leopoldo Lujan who served in the army. They had all died in 1968. One line behind and two to the right a headstone caught my eye. It had, in large letters a first name, a woman's name, my name: Corinne. I didn't stay to see what else it said.

Twelve

"When I stand by David's grave, it doesn't have the same impact it did years ago." Doug Westphall sat rigidly at the linoleum-topped table in his mobile home in Aurora, Colorado. "It's become more of a symbol. Of course, it's easier to accept his death now, but I still get bitter and angry and frustrated. Never as much as when he was lowered into the ground, though. That's a terrible moment."

It was a year since I had left the cemetery in Santa Fe. I had come back to the west, to find the tail-end of the story. It was mid-September; heat leaned against the closed windows that looked like thick venetian blinds, against the drawn polyester curtains. Denver smog drifted over Aurora, and I felt as though we were inside a sealed chamber.

I was curious to know Doug's reaction to the letter David

had written, warning him against the Marine Corps.

"I had dropped out of school at the time and was living at home. I had already been in Marine Platoon Leaders Class in school and was branded a maggot. I didn't think I could do anything.

"I was going to go to crop dusters school, but I didn't have the confidence I could fly the planes. David and Lynne were in Montana and I thought about going there, but I didn't go. I was going to try a pre-med course in Minnesota, but I didn't think I could handle it, so I dropped out. In Oklahoma I started at an aviation mechanics school but it was the same old thing. I would tell myself I couldn't do anything, so I'd stop whatever I was doing. I wandered around the country, running from everything."

I had brought a bottle of wine and we sat in the kitchen area, drinking from his two glasses. The floor was covered with avocado-colored plastic tiles; the stove and refrigerator were the same color, and the walls were lined with vinyl covering and green wallpaper. In the living area was a dark green couch and two chairs. There were no books, no pictures, no plants; there were no decorations or luxuries, except the TV and amplifiers which were both for sale. The mobile home, too, was for sale.

Earlier he had shown me the two bedrooms and the laundry room with its avocado-colored appliances. There were some files, a few clothes, and an empty carton that said Mr. Clean. In one of his letters he had referred to his "zoo-like existence."

We had arranged my visit by mail because he had no telephone. "I live frugally," he explained when I arrived, feeling ostentatious with my suitcases. "Since the air force, I've wasted a lot of time and squandered a lot of funds. I sold my life insurance and I'm living on that now. I don't believe my parents have much respect for me; I have been a great disappointment to them in nearly every way."

I asked if I could open a window. He looked surprised, but said it was all right. I pulled aside the curtains and looked out at the rows of mobile homes across the road, which was called Eisenhower Way, and which wound around the confine, the Aurora Friendly Village Mobile Home Court.

How far was it from the breakfast bar at Juan Tabo to wandering around the country, "running from everything"? To the hitchers with hard looks and lettered signs: L.A., Salt Lake, Santa Fe. The terrible discrepancy between people with cars and people without. Rock bottom in a motel with a mangled TV; light, and highway roar, hitting you before you wake. The way you can't escape seeing, in the mirror, how your jaw is set against the day. The sound of your voice cracking when you order coffee because the waitress is the first person you've spoken to since the afternoon before.

You go over and over, on paper napkins, the accounting of your funds—ones you brought and ones, if any, you left somewhere. You are less and less able to look a stranger in the eye. You see houses and tents full of families—people pulling together, you tell yourself, even when you see them screaming and splitting. You recall old loves, wonder if you should call—they may want you back, even though you wouldn't go. Maybe you should, though, maybe, you say, as you shake your head, no, to the worn-out kid who's begging you to buy his bugbitten sleeping bag.

It's not so far from the breakfast bar to the bottom line. But, then, the road is freedom, too. When Doug talked about wandering, it was as though it hadn't ended, and maybe never would. There was a look in his eyes—not what you'd call wanderlust, just a look that never seemed to settle anywhere, or on anything.

"The first time I flew an air force plane to Hawaii I felt better than I had in my whole life. I flew 'arc light' missions out of Okinawa and Thailand—refueling bombers on their way to Laos or Cambodia or Thailand. I never saw any bombs being dropped, but I saw a lot of craters in Vietnam. I always had qualms about flying aircraft that fueled bombers, but for some reason, I did it anyway. I have chastised myself, too, for *not* going to Vietnam, because of David. Maybe I should have gone."

It was easy to imagine him flying the gigantic tankers; his hands were steady as a stream. They floated reliably in his lap, or ferried his glass to and from his mouth, in a solid, reassuring manner. I believe that people have certain control centers in their bodies, centers that crack only with the final ravage or the final anger.

Doug Westphall had never made any trouble. His mother said: "When the boys were little I had to take David on a leash like a little doggie. Doug used to cling to my skirts." Another time, recounting some of David's boyhood illnesses, she said, "Nothing special ever happened to Doug."

I asked if he remembered that he had sometimes locked himself out of the house on the outskirts of Albuquerque when he was too little to go to school and his mother had gone to work. He said he didn't, but, later, when he went to make a call at a pay phone, and I said I was going to take a walk, he looked alarmed and admonished me not to lock myself out. I was sure he never forgot his keys.

His father had rarely mentioned him. "In general Dad was more tolerant and understanding of me than of David. Still, I remember one time when I was in high school, I had a muscle ailment and I went to bed with the bandage on because I was scared to rip it off. He got very upset with me so I got out of bed and ripped it off madly. Maybe it was a symbolic incident of how he felt I should have been. He felt I shouldn't have cared about the pain."

The mobile home was located directly between two airports. Planes flew overhead continuously. "You see," he said, "if my brother hadn't been killed, I would probably be a conservative person with a military career. The air force is very secure and financially rewarding.

"We got special pay if we were on hazardous duty. Before David's death I had trepidation about dying. Afterwards I didn't. I had a humanitarian deferment as a sole surviving son. Sometimes I took it, sometimes I didn't. When I flew in hazardous zones, I got more money and, also, I was able to get half-price stereo equipment for the chapel in Vietnam and Thailand.

"I regret not having had the wisdom to get out sooner. It took me a few years before I believed in the viewpoints of the people in the peace movement."

The summer after he got out of the air force he worked with his father at the chapel. Undoubtedly life on the knoll was different from inspirational feelings on the air base. Day–to–day chapel chores must have been grim. There had been too many dams, too many houses, too much building.

"Even at that time I realized that the chapel couldn't mean much. I saw people's casual reactions and I realized that few seemed affected by it."

Doug had, at the time, hopes and plans. Few of them had worked out. He had tried a computer programming course; he had thought of getting flight instructor ratings. He had contemplated going to medical school, but believed that, at thirty-four, he was too old. Finally, he applied to get back into the air force, as a health services administrator.

"You might ask yourself how in the hell I could feel the way I do about Vietnam, about American society and institutions, and still want to be part of the military. It's just that I see it as the least bad thing to do to meet my personal needs and also to have a chance to complete the chapel. With respect to the chapel, the military seemed like the *only* probable alternative."

Not long before I arrived in Aurora, he had been rejected by the air force.

"It is one of the most bitter disappointments of my life. I haven't found out yet specifically why I was rejected, but the chances are the selection board and the board's processes were pieces of shit."

But there was something else.

"In making my applications, it was necessary to explain the fact that I had declined a regular commission and had separated from active duty. That inevitably involved mention of David's combat death and of the chapel. I gave careful attention to an attempt to convince board reviewers that the chapel was strictly a patriotic effort. . . . What can I say?"

My head was reeling. I suggested that we walk around the encampment for a while. He seemed somewhat reluctant—maybe he didn't want the neighbors to see me, or to see him. I felt I was suffocating, though, so I insisted, and he opened the door to the bedlam of crickets.

As he closed and locked the door, he said, "The minute I bought this place I realized I didn't want it. I wished I hadn't bought it."

On one side of the home was a vacant lot in which a neighbor had planted a garden. Voluptuous sunflowers drooped their faces toward the ground; pumpkins, tomatoes, and corn made the lot a bright patch on the terrain. Behind the mobile home was a rise where the train shot by several times a day.

We walked slowly. Heat drifted off the metal roofs. All curtains were closed. Doug explained that most of the people who lived there were retired couples. No one was out. Planes took off and landed.

He walked beside me, stiffly. Handsome, small like his father, he always looks as though someone were about to attack him. His jaw in his heart-shaped face is always set. "I really don't know what to do about the chapel now."

"What would David say about it if he were alive?"

"He'd say, the chapel is fine, but what he would have wanted would be for my parents to have some happiness between themselves for their remaining years. He'd say, if you can get the money, do a limited number of things with the chapel—otherwise, forget it."

"It seems that you are doing that by trying to get it accepted as a national monument."

"That's true. At first we shied away from that approach, but what in hell is the point of struggling along the way we have been?"

I said I couldn't imagine.

"A few years ago I would have considered the chapel a failure if thousands of next of kin didn't send in photos and make changes in society. Now the only failure would be if it just didn't exist. Let's face it, though, the chapel has become an albatross."

An old man walked by with a dog and nodded. After we passed him, I looked back, and he had turned to stare at us. The dog sat on the asphalt beside his leg, panting.

"If my parents were dead, I'd make up tapes telling the truth as I see it and lock up the chapel and just have the tapes playing. You see, no matter what the chapel ever means, or ever stands for, it can never achieve what I want most—aside from life for those who died. I want revenge. For me the people who are responsible are Rostow, Westmoreland, dozens more like them—arrogant, pompous, elitist, egotistical, and contemptible maggots. The tapes would ask people if these pukes should be able to hide behind the defense that the American people supported them most of the time, when in fact the American people very likely would not have supported them if they had had access to the same evidence as that available to the leadership. The tapes would say that we were deceived into entering into Vietnam and into believing in it. That it was an attempt by the military to test the concept of counterinsurgency warfare. That the ultimate force behind it was the quest for economic hegemony."

I said that I would leave the tapes blank and let people record whatever they wanted to say. He looked at me as though he thought I was crazy.

We had completed the circle and we climbed back into the mobile home. I opened a few more windows and dropped back down at the table. My head was raging. He seemed impervious to the heat and to the incessant whine of airplanes.

He brought out some folders full of papers. He explained that the bill which Senator Domenici had introduced to Congress had been sent to the Advisory Board on National Parks, Historic Sites, Buildings and Monuments for consideration. That board concluded that it was neither "feasible nor desirable to establish the Vietnam Veterans Chapel as a unit of the National Park System." It contended that the chapel "does not possess national significance under the provisions of the Historic Sites Act of August 21, 1935," and that "the National Park Service presently administers no war memorials outside the National Capital area, other than those located in historic battlefield parks."

Doug, however, had established that there are, in fact, several war memorials outside the capital area which are not in historic battlefield parks. He showed me results of his research, said that he believed that certain monuments had received funding and had been accepted into the auspices of the government because of strong local pressures. In addition, one million dollars had recently been appropriated for the parking lot at the LBJ Memorial Grove on the Potomac.

"He has his space center, his library, his boyhood home park, and his grave. What did he need the Grove for? The

Grove was not supposed to cost the taxpayer anything. But if we pay for access to it, we have put some of our tax money into it. Someone said, 'Vietnam aside, LBJ was a great president.' I don't put Vietnam aside, and I don't think Johnson did either. I'm glad that his anguish over what he had such responsibility for probably killed the bastard. The point is that tribute is paid to the commander-in-chief, but not to his troops."

Although the board's recommendation cast a pall over the chapel project, Doug was determined to press for enactment of the bill. He spoke with inherited anger. "It would be unthinkable for my father to give up on the chapel. He's willing to spend weekends over there. Maybe it's not such a hardship on him. He should do what he can as long as it doesn't harm him. I think he realizes that the chapel can't change anything, but we want to keep it going. I would feel guilty if I had resources and didn't use them for the chapel."

"Why?"

"It's a matter of personal guilt. I'd feel guilty if there wasn't a memorial to the war dead."

Guilt, shame, sorrow, and anger had gone into the chapel as methodically as its mortar, stucco, wires, and stone. The builders were barricaded, now, inside its walls.

What would they do, I asked, if the bill did not pass? He looked so sad that I was sorry I had brought it up.

"Look," he said, "one has to choose between the sacrifice of ideas and the sacrifice of oneself. My father's life expectancy is sixteen years, my mother's twenty-one years, and mine forty years. How long should one sustain the memorial? If I have any heirs, I cannot justify saddling them with the responsibility *unless* a very adequate supply of money is available, so the long-range picture is very cloudy. I never thought I'd say this, but since I didn't get back into the air force, I've been thinking that total abandonment should be considered."

•   •   •

"In a way, it would be perfect if the chapel were abandoned. It would make an interesting ruin." Ted Luna, the man who designed the chapel, sat in a modern chair in his sunlit office in Santa Fe. "After all, the Vietnam vet has been forgotten. So has the war. We have short memories: 50,000 men gave their lives and we have nothing to say."

It was hard for me to imagine an architect so calmly contemplating the disintegration of his creation, but he spoke softly, his clear blue eyes sparkling with irony. "The stucco will deteriorate over the first twenty years. Eventually there will be various states of deterioration."

The chapel had been Ted Luna's second commission.

"It was conceived in fifteen minutes on a rainy morning. I wanted to do something that would have significance, to relate it to the time in history that forced it into existence and, also to give it a sense of timelessness. There is an ethereal quality to the Moreno Valley, there's a sense there that's not explicable. Timelessness is the major key for the design of the chapel. It is a space that beckons you to spend more time."

Behind him on the wall was a painting he had done of a huge hawk drifting against a white background. The painting was, somehow, reminiscent of the chapel.

"I made a model for the chapel and took it to the Westphalls at the ranch. They were sitting on the porch of the house. Victor just sat there and looked at it and then he began to cry. He said, 'That's beautiful.' It was one of those clear moments.

"Then we had a conversation about the mysticism of the area, about how doors were always slamming and things like that. The Westphalls were very susceptible to any variation from the norm.

"I always got along with them, though, and they never questioned my integrity. Victor has respect for anyone who is a professional. I was never on their list."

Ted Luna is part Spanish and part Indian. He grew up in New Mexico. When he talked about the chapel, I had the feeling that, if it was anyone's, it was his, precisely because he had let it go.

"Victor had decided to use David's insurance money for something significant. There was $30,000. He spent half on the mortgage payment for the ranch, and half on the chapel. I charged a 7 percent fee, so I made less than $2,000."

I listened carefully. I had never investigated the finances of the chapel, but I knew that in the proposal for making it into a national monument, total cost was listed as $54,700. Part of that—$37,500—was designated as "Westphall family funds." Ninety percent of total cost was listed as "used for actual construction and architect's fees." I had had the impression that all of David's money had been used for the chapel.

Ted Luna went on. "We hired a contractor and brought in a construction crew to do the foundation and structure. One time we were flying out of the ranch and there was a violent wind. The plane went into a spiral. We were trying to clear the pass, heading into the wind. We lost altitude in an abnormal way, turned back, spiraled again, and on the third try, we started across. We were 300 feet from the pass and we hit a downdraft, just cleared it at 100 feet. There were violent ultraviolet rays. It's a strange valley."

When CBS came to do a special on the chapel for national television, the helicopter which carried the film crew crashed in the valley. The pilot and cameraman survived with minor cuts, but the helicopter itself was demolished.

Ted Luna partially closed his eyes, remembering his days with the Westphalls. "The work crews had to be quartered in the other houses there because the Westphalls didn't trust them. There were constant animosities between them; for instance, they complained because the workmen hung their laundry outside to dry.

"But Victor was very dedicated to the project. He did all the finishing touches: the stucco, glazing, floor, and electrical system."

Again, I had had a different impression. I had thought that Ted Luna designed the chapel and the old man had, almost single-handed, built it. I had never heard of a contractor or construction crew. But, then, every story belongs to its teller, and, in the end, it may not matter.

"The area around Taos and the Moreno Valley has always been susceptible to strife and mysticism. It is conducive to energy forces, so I suppose you could say that indefinable forces are at work. The place reenforces supernatural feelings. I believe that the vibrations are good ones, except for the ranch house. I will never go back there. For me, it was ominous, and decadent.

"I designed the chapel with all this in mind. If you noticed, the door faces the Blue Lake, the Indian's sacred lake, as well as Wheeler Peak. I suppose that the justification for the chapel is simply that it is there."

I asked him if he had seen the lights on the chapel at night.

"The first time I saw them," he answered softly, "I stopped in the road. I couldn't even drive."

"They're gone now," I said. "Did you know?"

He said he hadn't known, and that he was sorry, but I could see that it was an abstract sorrow.

I had received a letter from the old man:

THE DAY THE LIGHTS WENT OUT

That's it. That's today—and the lights are those at the chapel. I should write an essay on the subject, but I have not the energy; besides, what would I do with it? Where would it do any good?

Contributions simply do not cover expenses. . . .

One of the most beautiful sights on earth is the Chapel lighted at night, yet those lights are going out.

Already, in less than a decade, the chapel had started its return, to the valley and the mountains, and to the regulations of the sky.

Thirteen

I went home, to the East, where I lived with my children in the house I bought when we had given up on New Mexico and moved away. The house was near a stream. My life may not have been much happier than it was in New Mexico, but I felt less isolated, less an interloper. My purposes had shifted away from tracking down tragedies and moved in the direction of raising my son and daughter— perhaps so that they could grow tall and strong and good. We could hear the stream all day and all night; we had a cat and a dog. I missed my cousin and the smell of piñon, the hum of her house, and the color of the New Mexican sky, but I was better off.

My last trip to the chapel, the year after I had visited David's grave, was less a pilgrimage than a duty. I was more interested in families than I was in monuments. I slept at my cousin's, borrowed her car, and drove toward Eagle Nest.

Sunlight struck at the glass door of the hut beside the chapel. I knocked and the old man got up from his armchair inside, squinting into the glare. He opened the door and held out his hand. "Hello," he spoke formally, "I'm Victor Westphall."

"It's Corinne!"

"Oh, Corinne, forgive me . . . I . . . I was working and I . . ."

"It's all right, it's all right." We went inside.

He looked flustered, like an aged wizard who had confused his lines. I babbled about the drive from Santa Fe, hoping to unembarrass him. In the year since I had seen him, his face seemed to have fallen into lines and spaces, like a puzzle made out of large pieces. His eyes looked drained, and he gestured at the place with brusque little movements. I felt as though I had invaded his lair.

"Forgive the mess . . ." He moved around, picking up, half-heartedly. His work table was piled with papers. "I'm at work on some plans for a solar-heated addition to our residence," he explained, pointing out a plan. Files surrounded his chair. "And I'm finishing up the land grant book. It has been brutally difficult, but should be rewarding when completed."

He tossed some jogging pants and a sweat shirt on the back of a chair. His sleeping bag lay open on the couch which was being used as a bed. A jockstrap lay on another chair. He pushed a beer can behind the table leg. Beside his armchair a bag of peanuts had spilled out onto the floor. I thought, he is happy here.

A manuscript entitled *Trial by Combat* sat on a shelf. He walked slowly to the kitchen and I followed him. In the back it was dark. The windows were too small to let in much light. He put the kettle on. Spread out on the counter were a package of American cheese, canned vegetables, more peanuts. It was sparse, but everything was his way.

I toured the room while he waited by the stove. It occurred to me that if Jeanne died, he would live here. And then, when his time came, Doug would live here, too. Would they be buried here? Tapes endlessly playing their voices, talking of an irreversible mistake and its eternal repercussions? I wondered if they had made arrangements. Who inherits a monument when the monument-maker dies?

He put Lipton tea bags in plastic cups and poured the water. He put sugar on the table and turned, peering into the room, as though he were looking for me. "Tea," he said.

He seemed to gain strength as he drank. He asked if I knew what had happened to Matt Hill. "He just left, you know; I never knew where he went." I said I didn't know. I didn't say that, several times, on several streets, I thought I had seen him. Boots, a shirt, hair curled a certain way. But, by then, I knew better, and I hadn't stopped to check.

He told me that his tooth condition was still bad, but that it wasn't hurting at the moment. He spoke gingerly, as though it did hurt, but that was undoubtedly a habit.

"This morning I did an easy five miles followed by eight 220's. Jeanne doesn't get out on the highway with me where I run, but she does walk and jog quite a bit around our house, and on the putting green. Incidentally, before I ran this morning, I did fifty knee lifts hanging from a bar followed by thirteen chins without dismounting, followed by three groups of fifty pushups in each group with some rest in between."

"Isn't that too much?"

"I don't think so, but I have the same pain," he pointed at his chest.

"You have to take care of yourself. You should go to a doctor."

"I have to keep going."

"But why, at such a price?"

"I have to keep going. I want to be prepared."

"For what?"

"You don't understand." He sighed and ironed the sleeve of his flannel workshirt with his hand which had grown simian with arthritis. "I want to be, theoretically anyway, ready."

"Ready for what?"

He asked if I had time to read something. I said I had all day. He got up and handed me his novel, said that if I read it I would understand.

I settled down with the book in the triangle of sunlight that came through the door. *Trial by Combat* was, as far as I knew, his first novel. I wondered when he had had time to write it. While I read, he went outside and started pounding away at the wall, repairing something that had gone awry.

Reading, I realized that he had written out his fantasy. The book is the story of Eric Masters, a retired Nebraska minister, seventy-nine years old, who is chosen to fight Chi–Huang, a Chinese scholar of the same age, in hand-to-hand combat, on Easter Island, in order to determine which country shall rule the world, and to avoid total destruction of the human race. Both men are killed, but Chi–Huang's vital signs last a little longer than Eric's.

As I read, I realized that he had written out his life.

Eric Masters "had always lived in the shadow of anonymity . . . he had never experienced anything to even remotely attach his name to other than a modest local fame. . . . He had volunteered because he thought it was the proper thing to do. . . . Was it vain of him to feel elated because he had kept himself in better-than-average physical condition? . . . He had always looked upon his body as something he occupied for a time—as a loan from God— and he had always considered it his Christian duty to keep that body in good condition. Moderation and discipline had been the credo of his life."

I realized that the book told more of his life than any of the talks I had had with him, or than any of the letters he had written to me. It was his way of telling his truth. It was his interpretation.

"He remembered that in his youth he had walked many a mile behind a horse–drawn, hand–held plow. This was the standard implement of agriculture in Biblical times and centuries before, yet in his lifetime it had become a museum piece in most of the world. . . . He had always tried to be helpful. He had genuinely gone out of his way to do more for others than he expected others to do for him."

There are several scenes in which Mrs. Masters is present. The woman's outstanding feature is that she never speaks. When news comes that Eric has been chosen to fight

Chi–Huang, "she looked at Eric for long moments as he sat with his elbows on the desk, staring ahead." And after the General comes to tell him what to do, "neither spoke as she glided silently into his arms."

The book, however, is not without a certain sympathy for the woman. "Eric knew why this whole matter was an especially arduous ordeal for her. In 1967, a similar scene had been enacted, only then it was their son and only child who had held his mother as he prepared to leave for Vietnam.

"Vietnam, that long-ago and far-off place that those without a special reason had tried so desperately to forget. But Eric and his wife . . . especially his wife . . . had not forgotten. Their son had died there. And now, the bitter memories of nearly three decades hung like a heavy cloud upon them as they silently consoled each other.

"This was a new burden heaped upon the old for the wife and mother. Never, never in her wildest imaginings could she have dreamed that she would be sending another warrior off to battle. . . . Could they not have had their remaining years together in peace? . . . But this they knew; the odds for the world, and that world's civilization, were no better (than his). And Eric would carry a banner for all the world to see."

I began to see what the old man had wanted, and what he had missed.

"The congratulations to Eric that followed were some of the most somber ever heard in the hallowed halls of Congress. The President, Cabinet, and members of Congress alike looked upon him with unrestrained awe. . . . Members of the press were clamoring to talk with him. . . . He would talk with them during his rest periods (from his morning run)."

I sensed what he feared.

"He had asked that a chinning bar be available. He had a special reason for this request. For nearly one half a century, he had gauged whether or not he was growing old by a simple test that was part of his daily routine . . . fifty knee lifts hanging from a bar, and ten chins without dismounting. Eric was aware that possibly not a single reporter would be able to duplicate this stunt, yet he saw no reason to alter his life-long routine, although he didn't want to embarrass the assemblage by asking anyone to try . . . and no one did, as they watched in open-mouthed amazement. . . . Now he launched into one that he had been following for the past few days. He started with a mile warmup jog, covering the four circuits of the track in about nine minutes . . . the newsmen . . . were strung out at various speeds behind him. . . . Others straggled up at various intervals during the five minute rest period.

"The major part of Eric's workout now followed: four distances of 660 yards in a little less than two and half minutes each. By this time reporters were strung out completely around the track, trying to gauge their pace as unobtrusively as possible so they would be somewhere in the vicinity when Eric stopped to walk . . . and talk.

"Eric finished his session with an easy half-mile jog. He had covered nearly four miles while alternately walking, jogging, and running . . . and he had given a twenty-five-minute press conference in the process, all with a perfectly straight face.

"While Eric was typically a serious man, he had quietly enjoyed this little prank. When it was over, though, he let it be known that it was just that—a prank . . . and then he talked amiably with the gentlemen of the press for over a full hour.

"In all, his was a thoroughly gentlemanly performance. By the time the interview was over, Eric had become nearly a legend in the eyes of the members of the Fourth Estate. He had proven himself the absolute antithesis of the standard concept for a man of his age as a senile incompetent struggling with a cane for mobility and mouthing cackled inanities. From what they wrote, the world would emphatically understand that this was no second-rate specimen of manhood that the United States was sending into the fray."

The difference between his book and his life was that, in life, the man had created his opponent. And the outcome of the battle had not been a draw.

I went outside to find him.

"Now do you understand?" he asked, shading his eyes from the sun. "It is not wholly unlikely that such a situation would arise. There really could come a day when two men might be chosen to step forward and fight to settle their countries' destinies. I would want to offer to go. That is why I want to be ready, why I have to be prepared."

I stood still. I knew I had heard him correctly. Was he, perhaps, right? Had it all come to that, had we come full circle and were we so overarmed that all we could do, in the end, would be to choose two old men to fight out our future?

We walked around and he pointed at the markers beside the round white stepping-stones. "We have more photos than markers now," he said sadly. "I can't keep up any-more." The wind flapped the rope on the flagpole. The old man's shirt blew around him, like the clothing on a scare-crow.

We went into the chapel and sat on the cold steps, the way we had when I first had come there. He said that he was having trouble keeping all the photos together. I tried to say something comforting, but he looked distraught and his words came out in a sort of cry. "I want all my boys to-gether!" Behind us, on the rough stucco, David stared out with an air of grim assurance I'm sure he thought was appropriate for the camera and the dress blues he was wearing. Still, the camera caught the fear and the questions that wouldn't leave his eyes.

He and I had had the same kind of illusions: I went to New Mexico to save myself; he went to Vietnam to save "those little people from Communism." We had found our elabo-rate and sanctified escapes. I had the arrogance to think that I could put down roots in a place I knew nothing about, simply because it was attached to the United States. I thought I could merge into a frontier community—it never occurred to me that no one wanted me. I was after the myth; David left New Mexico, full of zeal to export it. He believed he was going to help, to make a contribution to the world. He forgot that our problems are personal. He helped us push our borders into Cam Ranh Bay. But he died before it was clear that it didn't work, that it was the end of the frontier illusion.

The old man was speaking to me. He was saying that he had something he had to tell me.

"I woke up at 4:00 A.M. with my teeth aching violently, so I took a swallow of wine and tried to relax. I got back to sleep and awakened at about 6:30 with my teeth feeling as though the pain was masked. I had just been with David. I was seated on the edge of the bed at the chapel office and he was sitting in a chair opposite from me. He was playing his guitar, a fantastic instrument with unusual features including a delicate chain that hung over the strings to mute them in a certain way. Another innovation was a system of two buttons that, when pressed, evidently changed the chording arrangement in a subtle way. I asked him about these buttons and he started to speak, but only an unclear sound resulted. Then, as though realizing that the sound was discordant relative to the delicate clarity of the guitar music, and might set my teeth to resumed violent aching, he audibly, clearly, delicately, and shyly uttered the single word: Oops. I reached out to touch him with a gesture of compassionate understanding but he was gone, and I was awake."

I wondered if the old man understood that his book and his dream were telling him his story.

He said that Jeanne was waiting for him and he would have to be going. I said I would stay for a while and watch the sunset. He paused outside the chapel and looked at the sky. "If you have read *Trial by Combat* you know that Eric Masters would be seventy-nine in 1993. It turns out that I, too, will be seventy-nine in that year." He trudged off toward the flagpole, lowered the flag, folded it, and put it inside. He locked both buildings, shook my hand, and drove away.

•   •   •

I walked along the steppingstones, looking at the markers: Robert Harris from Kentucky; David F. Brown from Florida, broken in two and fallen off; Charles Kirkland from Missouri; and James R. Joshua from Alabama. There was a chill in the air and the sound of trucks down below. The mountains above Angel Fire turned mauve in the reflected sunset, but the color didn't brush the chapel. My feet crunched on the stones. A black cat jumped out of a barrel and mewed after me as though it were hungry.

I sat down and watched the cat. A dusty blue Chevy station wagon drove up the drive. A man and his son got out and walked along the steps. He had left the engine running, and his wife and two other children stayed in the car. Trash was falling out of the trash can in the parking lot, and one of the kids threw a popsicle wrapper out the window. Below, the valley stretched out tan and dry and covered with withering camomile.

The station wagon went away and a jet streak began in the west, climbed higher and higher until it hung over the valley. The sky was filled with luminescence, like the color of Roman glass, and the sun went down behind the ranch. The wind stopped, at its mysterious interval, and then began to blow again.